Vetting and Monitoring Employees

Vetting and Monitoring Employees

A Guide for HR Practitioners

GILLIAN HOWARD

Routledge
Taylor & Francis Group
LONDON AND NEW YORK

First published 2006 by Gower Publishing

Reissued 2018 by Routledge
2 Park Square, Milton Park, Abingdon, Oxon, OX14 4RN
711 Third Avenue, New York, NY 10017, USA

Routledge is an imprint of the Taylor & Francis Group, an informa business

A Library of Congress record exists under LC control number: 2005035226

ISBN 13: 978-0-815-39887-5 (hbk)
ISBN 13: 978-1-351-14340-0 (ebk)

Contents

CHAPTER 1

Introduction

GENERAL LEGISLATIVE FRAMEWORK

The laws relating to employers' rights to monitor the use of the internet and email, monitor and record telephone calls, secretly record their movements whether at work or out of work and discipline them for breach of the rules, are complex and wide-ranging. Here are some of the most important:

- The Regulation of Investigatory Powers Act 2000 (RIPA) outlaws, except in certain circumstances, employers' rights to monitor, inspect and record emails, internet use and telephone calls at work.
- The Telecommunications (Lawful Business Practice) (Interception of Communications) Regulations 2000 (Lawful Business Regs) provide 'gateways' through which employers may *lawfully* monitor and record their employees' calls, emails and internet use.
- Data Protection Act 1998 (DPA) and Codes of Practice (four parts) provide the framework for employees' rights not to have personal data about them misused or disclosed by their employer to unauthorised sources.
- Computer Misuse Act 1990 makes it a criminal offence to 'hack in' to data held on computers.
- Protection from Harassment Act 1977 makes it a criminal offence to stalk or otherwise harass someone.
- Equal opportunities legislation that is, Sex Discrimination Act 1975; Race Relations Act 1976; Disability Discrimination Act 1995; Employment Equality (Religion or Beliefs) Regulations 2003; Employment Equality (Sexual Orientation) Regulations 2003 outlaw discrimination on these grounds.
- Employment Rights Act 1996 (ERA) in this context regulates the fairness or otherwise of dismissals.
- Defamation Act 1996 defines defamation and includes corporate liability for information transferred via the internet and other electronic means and the permitted defences.

- Human Rights Act 1998 – in this context we refer to Article 8 the right to respect for private and family life and correspondence; Article 9 the Freedom of Thought, Conscience and Religion and Article 10 the Freedom of Expression.
- Obscene Publications Acts 1959 and 1964 define 'obscenity' and make it a criminal offence to publish material that has a tendency to deprave or corrupt persons.
- The Telecommunications Act 1984 makes it a criminal offence to send any indecent, menacing or obscene message through the public telecommunication system.
- Protection of Children Acts 1978 and 1999 make it a criminal offence to take or distribute indecent photographs of children and provide for a register of persons unsuitable to work with children.
- Public Interest Disclosure Act 1998 now S43A of ERA protects employees who make 'protected disclosures' that is, who are whistleblowers on fraud and other matters.

Employers are potentially at risk for a wide range of civil and criminal offences. Understanding the legal complexities of monitoring and recording workers' telephone calls and reading their emails, investigating their use of the internet, using covert surveillance on them and the introduction of practical policies which are well known to all staff and workers on site, should help in navigating these difficult waters.

As Lord Denning once said about the Treaty of Rome 1957 (now the Treaty of Maastricht 1992) 'the Treaty is like an incoming tide. It cannot be held back…'.

It is important for employers and employees to understand these legal liabilities and their duties and obligations. Below we summarise a few of the important legal and 'cyber' definitions.

HISTORY

The Security Service in the UK (commonly known as MI5) has had a long and colourful history operating since the beginning of the twentieth century monitoring and vetting devices in order to safeguard national security. In 1909 Captain Vernon Kell of the Army and Captain Mansfield Cumming of the Royal Navy formed the Secret Service Bureau (SSB) which was then split into two arms – one headed by Kell called 'K' who was in charge of counterespionage at home and the other arm 'C' headed by Captain Mansfield

Cumming responsible for obtaining intelligence abroad. This latter activity is now performed by MI6 (in which the famous fictional spy James Bond served). Other departments under the Directorate of Military Intelligence under which the SSB came in 1916 were those such as code-breaking, aerial reconnaissance, propaganda and censorship.

Today MI5 employs around 1900 staff and has four main functions – to carry out espionage, counteract terrorism, combat serious crime and the vetting of certain foreign nationals who come to the UK to study at university as British universities have access to and help develop modern technology.

Civil servants are subject to positive vetting (PV) since January 1952 when the Government of the day decided to introduce a procedure 'for ensuring the reliability of government staff employed on exceptionally secret work, especially work involving access to the secret information about atomic energy'.

This included obtaining oral and written references from those well known to the individual in their private life, their close relatives, the organizations and associations to which the individual belongs. At least two referees must fall into this category as well as references from employers.

ELECTRONIC TAGGING

Some employers are even using electronic tagging to monitor the whereabouts and the work output of their staff.

The General and Municipal Boilermakers' Union (GMB) has reported that workers in warehouses and distribution centres are being required to wear microcomputers fitted to their bodies.

This electronic tagging is supposed to reduce costs and increase efficiency. It works by way of a satellite which beams the radio waves to a central station where the employee can be monitored.

A very interesting article on this matter has been written by Jeffrey Jupp at 7 Bedford Row, 'Tagging – a technology too far?', in July/August 2005 edition of *Employment Law Journal*.

CHAPTER 2

The Law on Monitoring Telephone Calls and Emails and Internet Regulation

INTRODUCTION

There is no reason why employers should not lawfully monitor their employees both for business reasons and to protect themselves from liability under the anti-discrimination legislation and the laws of defamation. Employers are vicariously liable for the acts of their employees committed in the course of employment – both at common law and under the anti-discrimination legislation (s.41 of the Sex Discrimination Act 1975; s.32 of the Race Relations Act 1976, s.58 of the Disability Discrimination Act 1995, Regulations 22 of the Employment Equality (Sexual Orientation) Regulations 2003 and Employment Equality (Religion or Belief) Regulations 2003) as well as for defamation. This is because of the relationship of Principal and Agent rather than on the basis of vicarious liability.

An employer is vicariously liable for negligent acts or omissions of their employees acting in the course of employment, whether or not such act or omission was specifically authorised by the employer. To avoid vicarious liability, an employer must demonstrate either that the employee was not negligent in that the employee was reasonably careful or that the employee was 'on a frolic of their own' rather than on the employer's business.

It is rare for the courts or tribunals to find an employee on a frolic of their own. In one case where employees committed racist or sexually offensive acts, branding a black colleague and calling him 'chimp', 'monkey' and 'baboon' (*Jones* v *Tower Boot Co Ltd* [1997] IRLR 168 Court of Appeal), the Court held that the employer remained firmly fixed with vicarious liability even though the employees concerned were not employed to brand their colleagues or to make offensive racist statements.

STATISTICS

According to *Personnel Today* on 9 July 2002, 25 per cent of dismissals concern the misuse of the internet and of those, 69 per cent relate to downloading pornography. Cyberskiving, that is, employees wasting their work time on the internet, was also high on the list of complaints by employers with 40 per cent of companies referring to this issue in the survey and 9 per cent of these complaints concerned discriminatory emails.

REASONS WHY EMPLOYERS MAY WISH TO MONITOR AND RECORD COMMUNICATIONS AT WORK

Firstly, for sound business reasons the employer may wish to monitor and control what employees are writing or saying by telephone. Legally binding contracts can be formed either orally or in writing by email.

Secondly, some dishonest employees may try to disclose or 'sell' confidential information or may be involved in other dishonest activities, using the telephone or email system at work to do so.

Thirdly, employees who post defamatory notices on websites, orsending offensive or libellous emails (sometimes with offensive attachments downloaded from the internet) can lead to serious legal penalties for the employer.

Fourthly, there may be health and safety reasons for example, where workers work alone or in isolated locations.

Fifthly, employers may seek to protect their workers and customers by recording telephone calls (to ensure that there is a faithful record of what has been said) and monitoring emails in order to prove whether an order was sent and received and so on, if done by email.

THE LAW

There are several statutes and sets of regulations and a Data Protection Code of Practice regulating the legality of monitoring and/or recording telephone calls, emails and the internet at work and using closed-circuit television (CCTV) to record and monitor the activities of those at work.

RIPA

The Regulation of Investigatory Powers Act 2000 (RIPA) was enacted in 2000 as part of the UK's response to Article 5 of the Telecommunication Data Protection Directive (EU 97/66). The Directive established the basic principle that communications cannot be intercepted unless there are reasonable grounds for believing that both the sender and the intended recipient have consented to the interception.

The Act established a legal framework for carrying out surveillance and other forms of intelligence gathering.

The Act created criminal offences in connection with the unlawful interception of communications on a public or private telecommunication systems and a civil offence based on the tort of unlawful interception of telecommunications. A civil action can lead to an injunction restraining the unlawful interception and/or damages for any financial loss suffered

The Act therefore covers telephone conversations, faxes, emails and internet communications. Video surveillance or other forms of covert surveillance may be covered depending upon the system used.

The only exclusion would be a free-standing intranet (internal company) system, not connected to a public telephone network.

Mobile and wireless application protocol (WAP) telephones are also not covered by the Act.

THE REGULATIONS

The Telecommunications (Lawful Business Practice) (Interception of Communications) Regulations 2000 - SI 2000/2543 (the Regs) provide 'gateways' through which employers may lawfully monitor telephone calls and so on.

DATA PROTECTION

The Data Protection Act 1998 (DPA) and in particular Part 3 of the Code of Practice published under the Data Protection Act 1998 covers any personal data and gives individuals at work additional protection from unlawful 'snooping'. The Code of Practice (Part 3) gives guidance to employers as to how they may lawfully monitor calls, faxes and emails and so on, and use covert surveillance.

THE HUMAN RIGHTS ACT 1998 (HRA)

The HRA provides, under Article 8(1) for the 'right to respect for an individual's private life, family life and correspondence'.

GUIDANCE

THE HOME OFFICE

The Home Office has produced its guidance on covert surveillance for the purposes of Regulation of Investigatory Powers Act 2000.

OFTEL

OFTEL's guidance covers the recording of telephone calls.

THE REGULATION OF INVESTIGATORY POWERS ACT 2000 (RIPA)

RIPA reflects the changes which have taken place in the communications industry over the last 15 years. It also ensures that the UK's interception regime is compliant with Article 5 of the Telecommunication Data Protection Directive EU 97/66 which requires member states to protect the confidentiality of communications.

The basic principle is that communications may not be intercepted unless there are reasonable grounds for believing that both the sender and intended recipient have consented to the interception.

The Telecommunications (Lawful Business Practice) (Interception of Communications) Regulations 2000 take advantage of the scope allowed by the Telecommunication Data Protection Directive for member states to limit the general prohibition on interception *without consent* in order to ensure that businesses may record or monitor communications to obtain evidence of transactions or other business communications.

RIPA replaces the previous relevant law (Interception of Communications Act 1985) and creates new offences of unlawful interception on public and private telecommunications systems and a tort of interception on private systems by those who run them.

Monitoring (and tapping) of incoming and outgoing telephone calls, faxes and emails on a public telephone system will be illegal except (importantly) as permitted by the Regulations or under a warrant issued by the Secretary of State (see below).

FRAMEWORK

The basic principle is that *communications may not be intercepted unless there are reasonable grounds for believing that both the sender and intended recipient have consented to the interception.*

However, the Act establishes a legal framework to govern the interception of communications in the course of their transmission on public or private telecoms systems. The purpose of the Regulations (see below) is to make sure that legitimate business practices are not prevented by the Act.

Part II regulates techniques such as use of agents/informants used by law enforcement, security and intelligence agencies. In view of the provisions of the Human Rights Act 1998, the previous non-statutory authorization system would have been inadequate and was therefore replaced.

Part III provides power for the government to require any person to provide a plain text copy of any encrypted information.

Part IV provides for codes of practice and supervisory commissioners.

BACKGROUND

RIPA updated the law on the interception of communications to take account of technological change such as the growth of the internet.

It also puts other intrusive investigative techniques on a statutory footing for the very first time. It provides new powers to help combat the threat posed by rising criminal use of strong encryption and ensures that there is independent judicial oversight of the powers in the Act.

The Home Secretary Jack Straw said:

> *The Regulation of Investigatory Powers Act 2000 (RIPA) will ensure that the UK's law enforcement and security agencies have the powers they need to do their job effectively in a changed technological world. New communications tools such as the Internet offer up huge legitimate benefits for us all. But serious criminals too have always been quick to jump on the latest technological bandwagon in their efforts to evade detection. The "e" prefix can apply to today's criminals as well as to commerce. RIPA will play a vital role in combating this very real threat. In updating law enforcement powers, we have been careful to see that individuals' rights are properly protected. We recognise that powers such as interception are intrusive. That is precisely why they should be very closely regulated. RIPA ensures that this is the case. And it also*

ensures that other traditional law enforcement techniques – such as the use of agents – are, for the very first time, subject to proper statutory controls and safeguards. We have also listened to industry's views throughout the passage of the legislation and made changes as a result. This is all about a balance. We believe that RIPA strikes the right one. This is an important Act. And not just for those who are hooked up to the Internet now. We all have an interest. The RIPA powers, simply put, are essential to help keep the UK a safe place for everyone to live and work.

CONSENT

The easiest way for employers to intercept communications lawfully is to obtain the consent of the employees. This can be done in the contract and by inserting a provision in the staff handbook making it clear that by signing acceptance of the handbook the employee agrees that their telephone, email and internet access can be monitored and recorded by the employer.

They could also be required under the terms of their contract to inform family and friends and all third parties to whom they telephone, email and write and who may return calls, emails and letters. However, it is unlikely that in law an employee could give consent on behalf of their family and friends. Even if under RIPA such express consent could be obtained via the employee, there would still be problems under the Data Protection Act 1998 and Human Rights Act 1998 (see later chapters).

THE DETAIL

The Telecommunications (Lawful Business Practice) (Interception of Communications) Regulations 2000 (the 2000 Regulations) authorize employers to monitor and record employees' telephone calls, emails and internet use without their consent.

The provisions of RIPA and the 2000 Regulations which came into force on 2 and 24 October 2000 respectively made it unlawful for an employer to intercept a *communication in the course of its transmission* by means of a *private telecommunication* (see below under 'Definitions') unless:

- both the maker or sender and the intended recipient of the communication have consented to its interception, or the interceptor has 'reasonable grounds' for believing that they have so consented (see 'Unauthorised interceptions' p. 15); or

- the interception is authorised by the Telecommunications (Lawful Business Practice) (Interception of Communications) Regulations 2000 ('the Regulations'), (see 'Authorised interceptions' p. 12).

In order to rely upon the exception to the rule about obtaining consent, the interception in question has to be 'business-related'. So eavesdropping on a private telephone call or reading a private email is unlawful.

PERSONAL EMAILS

How would an employer know it was a personal email unless he reads it? The Information Commissioner's view is that employers' policies should clearly set out whether and in what circumstances personal emails may be sent and received without interference from the employer.

The Code further advises that staff should be made aware of the content of such policies. If an organization allows limited personal use of the email system, the Code of Practice advises that the use of a marking system – to help protect private or personal communications – is encouraged and that, where possible, opening emails that clearly show they are private or personal communications is avoided.

Where email monitoring is taking place to detect malicious software, the Code of Practice points out that this can be achieved by the use of automated tools that check for suspicious codes without the need for an employer to actually open and read an email.

DEFINITIONS

A 'communication' includes 'anything comprising speech, music, sounds, visual images or data of any description' (s.81 (1)), and will be treated as being transmitted when it is being stored on the system in a way that enables the intended recipient to collect or otherwise have access to it (s.2(7)). This means that an interception takes place, for example, where an email message stored on a web-based service provider is accessed so that its contents are made available to someone other than the sender or intended recipient.

A 'private telecommunication system' is defined as any telecommunication system which is not a public telecommunication system but is attached to such a system. This means that an office network, linked to a public telecommunication system by a private telephone exchange, is to be treated as a private system. Interception of information in such a system other than by the system controller or with his consent is a criminal offence. An entirely self-standing system, on the other hand, such as a secure office intranet, does not fall within the definition.

How many secure office intranet systems are there which are not also linked to the outside telephone network?

'Interception' – A person intercepts a communication in the course of its transmission by means of a private telecommunication system if he or she 'so modifies or interferes with the system or its operation...so as to make some or all of the contents of the communication available, while being transmitted, to another person other than the sender or intended recipient of the communication' (s.2(2)).

A 'modification' of the system includes the attachment of any apparatus to, other modification of or an interference with, any part of it (s.2(6)(a). 'Modification' includes alterations, additions and omissions, and 'apparatus' includes any equipment, machinery or device and any wire or cable (s.8i(i)).

Any 'contents of a communication will be treated as being made available while being transmitted where they are diverted or recorded while being transmitted so as to be available to a person subsequently' (s.2(8)).

AUTHORISED INTERCEPTIONS

The Regulations made under s. 4(2) of RIPA authorise an employer (or someone else with its express or implied consent) to intercept, monitor and record the contents of a communication in the course of its transmission by means of a telecommunication system whose operation or use it has a right to control *without the consent* of the sender or intended recipient, for the following purposes:

(i) to establish the existence of facts (Regulation 3(a)(i)(aa)).

This would allow employers to intercept, read and monitor, faxes, emails and telephone calls where it was necessary to provide evidence of contractual negotiations or other business communications in case of disputes arising. This would also cover negotiating over changes to a contract. What is not clear is whether this covers the interception of emails or calls which form the basis of a disciplinary case. Certainly where there was a dispute over what had been agreed by email or by telephone, then it would be lawful to intercept the said emails or telephone calls to prove those facts.

(ii) to ascertain compliance with 'regulatory or self-regulatory practices or procedures that apply to the employer, or another person supervised by the employer in respect of those practices or procedures in the carrying on of their business' (Reg 3(1)(a)(i)(bb).

For example, the FSA and other self-regulatory bodies monitor calls to ensure that a trader (or other individuals) are complying with the regulatory body's own regulations and rules.

'Any self-regulatory practice or procedures' would include an employer's code of business ethics or a professional body's such as the General Medical Council's or the Law Society's or Bar Council's. It is debatable whether this 'gateway' would apply to the Equal Opportunities Commission's or Commission for Racial Equality's Equal Opportunities Codes of Practice as they possibly do not relate to 'the conduct of business'.

There are similar doubts over the Advisory, Conciliation and Advisory Service's (ACAS) Codes of Practice.

> *(iii) to ascertain or demonstrate the standards which are or ought to be achieved by persons using the system in the course of their duties (Reg 3(1)(a)(i)(cc).*

This exemption would, for example, cover customer call monitoring for quality control, performance monitoring in call centres and staff training purposes.

> *(iv) in the interests of national security (Reg 3(i)(a)(ii).*

> *(v) to prevent or detect crime (such as fraud or corruption) (Reg. 3(1)(a)(iii)).*

This would include employers' interception, for example, of telephone calls and emails for the purposes of detecting or preventing acts such as dishonesty or fraud. This would include cases of suspected fraud on the sick pay scheme, for example, fraudulent malingerers on sick leave.

> *(vi) to investigate or detect the unauthorised use of that or any other telecommunication system (Reg 3(1)(a)(iv)).*

For example, employers may wish to check that employees are not using the internet for purposes that are prohibited by the employer's policy on internet use.

Employers need to make it clear in their handbook or policy documents what constitutes authorised use of the telephone, email and internet and what does not (see Chapter 4).

> *(vii) to secure the effective operation of the system (Reg 3(1)(a)(v)).*

It is legitimate for employers to monitor and record emails, for example, to protect the system against viruses and hackers and to make routine interceptions for operational purposes such as backing up.

'Authorised interceptions' must take place on the employer's premises, or somewhere else under the control of either the employer or a person contracted to provide telephone services to the employer, and not during the transmission of the communication on a public network.

The people who use a system are, according to the Department of Trade and Industry's (DTI) *Notes for Business*, those who make direct use of it (that is, in the case of an employer's system, its employees). Someone who calls from outside, or who receives a call outside, using another system is *not* a user of the system on which the interception is made, for example, WAP or other form of mobile telephone.

Employers may need to consider others means of ensuring that mobile telephones are not used for unlawful purposes. For example, in investment banks, traders are banned from using mobile telephones on the trading floor as all calls have to be recorded under the Financial Services Authority's Conduct of Business 3.7.1.

MONITORING BUT NOT RECORDING

An employer may also monitor, but not record, communications:

- that are intended to be received by an employer (whether or not he or she has actually received them) to determine whether or not they relate to its business. For example, an employer may check an employee's voicemail box in his or her absence from work for business-related messages (Reg 3(1)(b) and (2)(d)(ii)); or
- made to confidential counselling or support help-lines which are free of charge (other than the cost of making the call) and guarantees callers anonymity (for the purposes of supporting or protecting the helpline staff) (Reg 3(1)(c)).

LAWFUL MONITORING AND RECORDING – MAKING REASONABLE EFFORTS TO INFORM STAFF

Monitoring and/or recording is authorised if:

- the communication relates to the employer's business or otherwise takes place in the course of that business being carried on, that is, not personal calls or personal emails of staff (Reg 3(2)(a));
- the system in question is provided for use wholly or partly in connection with that business (s.4(3) and Reg (3)(2)(b)).It would

therefore be lawful for an employer to listen to a voicemail message or open an employee's email in the employee's absence. Employees must, however, be aware of this and where possible give consent.

- the employer '*has made all reasonable efforts to inform every person who may use the telecommunication system in question, that communications transmitted on it may be intercepted*' (Reg 3(2)(c)).

This would cover both the employee and anyone who wished to communicate with them. Therefore at the very least all staff must be made aware that such interceptions may take place.

Employers could send an email to all staff informing them of the interception practices and regularly update the email on the internal system, reminding staff about this.

Employers could also insert a clause in the contract of employment informing staff that calls are monitored and in some cases recorded and have this as part of the email and internet policy in the handbook.

For the interception to be lawful it also has to be *'necessary'*, i.e. 'essential'.

UNAUTHORISED INTERCEPTIONS

Employers who wish to monitor or record the contents of a communication for purposes outside the scope of the Regs (such as marketing or marketing research) will have to have 'reasonable grounds' to believe that they have consent to the interception of both the sender and the intended recipient of the communication.

SO HOW WOULD EMPLOYERS DO THIS?

Employers could include a clause in the contract of employment whereby employees agree to their telephone calls and emails being monitored or recorded and instruct the call operator (or the employee) to ask outside callers at the start of the call whether or not they consent to its being monitored or recorded. Alternatively, a recorded message could be played to outside callers immediately their call is connected stating that their call will be monitored or recorded.

PRECEDENT

An example of a clause in the contract of employment is given below:

> *The Company operates an open and transparent email and internet policy. Because of the nature of our business we need to ensure that*

employees act with the utmost integrity. We therefore reserve the right to and in fact do, monitor and record telephone calls made to and from the company's offices.

It is a requirement of your contract that you advise everyone whom you telephone that the call is recorded for quality assurance and security reasons. We will respect private calls when they are made and will delete recordings of any private calls except where there is a legitimate reason not to do so.

It will be important that the outside caller is given a clear choice to refuse consent and to continue with the call, without it being monitored or recorded.

CIVIL LIABILITY

Employers will be liable for a civil tort of unlawful interception. The remedy is an injunction and/or damages.

CHAPTER 3

Monitoring Telephone Calls

INTRODUCTION

Nowadays there are various ways in which employers can monitor the telephone calls made and received at their business premises. These range from monitoring the telephone numbers to which outgoing calls are made and the duration of those calls to full tape-recordings of all external conversations conducted on telephones at business premises.

Monitoring can be for selected numbers, extensions only or all telephones at the business premises. Monitoring of selected numbers or extensions is particularly useful where competitive activity is suspected.

The tape-recording of all external telephone conversations is an option and it is common in certain types of business such as stockbroking and foreign exchange dealing where much of the business is conducted by telephone, instructions received have to be acted on more or less immediately and considerable sums of money may be at stake. Some employers regard any sort of monitoring as unacceptable but it can prove useful, for example, in detecting employees actively competing with their employer.

Employers who adopt any sort of monitoring need to decide what, if anything, they tell their employees about it.

There is no legal duty on the employer to inform the employee. However, the Office of Telecommunications (OFTEL), the UK regulator for the telecommunications industry, and now called the Office of Communications (OFCOM), has published guidance on monitoring telephone calls and this is produced at the end of this chapter.

ADMISSIBILITY IN COURT

The fact that the employer has not informed the employee in advance, should not, of itself, affect the admissibility of the recording in civil proceedings, but will mean ordinarily that the tapes may not be produced in evidence by the employer unless, in respect of each conversation, they can be 'proved' by direct oral evidence by the person who made each of the statements, or someone who heard them made, apart from exceptional circumstances provided for under s.4 of the Civil Evidence Act 1968.

In one case, secret tape-recordings had been made on behalf of the underwriters, of conversations between individuals involved in a conspiracy to blow up a ship and claim the loss from the insurance company

The appeal was on behalf of the underwriters, against a refusal to admit tape recordings under s.10(1)(c) Civil Evidence Act 1968, which were explained by written, out-of-court statements, made by a person who could not be present in court, because he was detained abroad.

The Court of Appeal held that the tapes, made without the knowledge of the person whose statements were being recorded, could only be 'proved' by someone who had heard the statements being made. In other words, a person who was actually present when the tape recordings had been made, had to come to Court to give oral evidence that those conversations took place on the days in question and that the witness giving the evidence had heard those conversations.

Statements made with the speaker's knowledge and intention are admissible under s.2 of that Act. The recorded statements made by the witness himself were also admissible.

The appeal was allowed in part.

CRIMINAL PROCEEDINGS

The Regulation of Investigatory Powers Act 2000 (RIPA) does not cover covert listening devices in a motor car which record a voice speaking on a mobile telephone. This is because it is not *'an interception of a communication in the course of transmission by means of a telecommunications system'*. It is therefore admissible as evidence in either civil or criminal proceedings – *R* v *E* (Admissibility of Covert Listening Device, reported in the Times Law Reports (TLR), 27 May 2004).

The Court of Appeal Criminal Division held that under Regulation of Investigatory Powers Act 2000 the critical words were in section 2(2) 'in the course of transmission'. The natural meaning of the word 'interception' denoted some form of interference with or obstruction of the signal being transmitted. The recording of a voice speaking on a telephone did not become 'interception' simply because what was said was not only recorded, but was transmitted by a separate process.

In addition, in criminal proceedings, s.17(1) of the Regulation of Investigatory Powers Act 2000 did not prevent any evidence being adduced, questions asked, assertions or disclosures made in order to ascertain whether a telecommunication system was a public or private system, irrespective of whether the evidence or questioning related to events prior to the implementation of the Act – Attorney-General's Reference (No 5 of 2000) House of Lords (HL), TLR, 18 October 2004.

This is an important part of the ruling as new laws are not retrospective and the court could have ruled that the retrospective rule applied to events that happened prior to the enactment of Regulation of Investigatory Powers Act 2000. It did not.

In this case the House of Lords added that it was also permissible in criminal proceedings, where an interception had taken place on a private system, to ask questions or adduce evidence to establish that the interception had been carried out by or for the person with the right to control the operation or use of the system, where the interception took place before the implementation of the 2000 Act and also, subject to the facts of the case, after the implementation of the Act.

In this case police officers were suspected of supplying confidential and sensitive information to, among others, a known criminal.

Telephones used by them were tapped between 1996 and 1997 with the consent of the chief constable, under the Interception of Communications Act 1985.

Prior to the trial in 2002, after the 2000 Act came into force, the Crown served expert evidence on the defendant to show that the interception had taken place on a private telecommunications system.

The defence alleged that the interception had taken place on a public telecommunications system and that by virtue of s.17(1) of the 2000 Act, investigation into the circumstances of the interception was prohibited. The House of Lords held that:

> *The 2000 Act was introduced to cover the whole field of interception; Parliament sought to make good the deficiency identified in Halford's case (see Chapter 8 on Human Rights) by regulating tapping of private telephones.*
>
> *It did not do so by prohibiting such interception altogether, but interception by a public authority had to be regulated by law and the subject of the interception, if it was unjustified, had to have a civil remedy (s.1(3)). The 2000 Act preserved all the essential features of the warrant regime established by the 1995 Act. There was nothing in the 2000 Act or other materials shown to the House to suggest a Parliamentary intention to*

> *render inadmissible as evidence any material which had previously been admissible save to the extent explained below, with regard to s1(2) and 17(2).*
>
> *The European Convention on Human Rights permitted necessary and proportionate interference with the right to respect for privacy guaranteed in Article 8(1) – see Article 8(2).*
>
> *... Given the obvious public interest in admitting probative evidence which satisfied the requirements of ss.1(6), 3 and 4 and the absence of any public interest excluding it, a court might properly enquire whether the interception was of a public or private system and if the latter, whether the interception was lawful'*

RECORDINGS ALLOWED IN EMPLOYMENT TRIBUNALS AND INTERNAL DISCIPLINARY HEARINGS

Tapes can and often have been produced at internal disciplinary hearings and employment tribunals, where the rules of evidence are not so strict. Indeed, in internal disciplinary and grievance hearings, tape-recordings may prove decisive.

In the Employment Tribunal case of *Mezzotero* v *BNP Paribas,* Case Nos: 2201221/2003 & 2203101/2003, a tape-recording of Ms Mezzotero's grievance against the bank's failure to allow her to return to her job following the birth of her second baby was taken in secret by Ms Mezzotero.

At the beginning of the grievance hearing, the two supposedly independent members of management hearing the grievance, the deputy head of Human Resources, Gill Somerset and Global head of Credit, David Ovenden, both used the pronoun 'we', when referring to the fact that the bank had concluded that no discrimination had taken place. The Employment Tribunal (apart from being surprised at such references to 'we') criticized both individuals, finding that they had come to the grievance hearing 'with closed minds' having already determined the issue without listening to Ms Mezzotero or testing the denials of the members of senior management.

The Employment Tribunal allowed these secret tape-recordings into evidence and for Ms Mezzotero to rely on them. This was in part because the Bank (through its officers) had been found not to have told the truth at meetings and during conversations in which they had not known they were being taped. Since credibility of the witnesses is critical where there is a dispute of fact, these tape recordings were also useful and determinative of the credibility of the witnesses generally.

THE PRIVILEGE AGAINST SELF-INCRIMINATION

Where a telephone call includes material that would incriminate the individual in either civil proceedings or criminal prosecution, they may be entitled to claim the privilege against self-incrimination.

Recently, an Employment Tribunal chairman was reminded of this privilege by Ms Carol Davis of Littleton Chambers, acting for the Respondents in an alleged unfair dismissal case, Here the Claimant had made an admission to a serious matter of housing fraud during the internal disciplinary hearing, which was taped (openly).

The prosecution was pending in the magistrates' court when the case came before the Employment Tribunal. The Chairman was reminded that the claimant was unrepresented and risked making admissions in the tribunal that could incriminate her in her future criminal proceedings. She had pleaded 'not guilty' to the charges. The case was therefore adjourned *sine die* until the outcome of the prosecution. The Chairman thanked Ms Davis for drawing this matter to his attention (*Oladeji* v *London & Quadrant Housing Trust* Case No: 3300941/2003).

The privilege against self incrimination in civil proceedings is subject to the provisions of the Civil Evidence Act 1968, s. 14 of which provides:

> *(1) The right of a person in any legal proceedings other than criminal proceedings to refuse to answer any question or produce any document or thing if to do so would tend to expose that person to proceedings for an offence or for the recovery of a penalty-*
>
> *(a) shall apply only as regards criminal offences under the law of any part of the United Kingdom and penalties provided for by such law; and*
>
> *(b) shall include a like right to refuse to answer any question or produce any document or thing if to do so would tend to expose the husband or wife of that person to proceedings for any such criminal offence or for the recovery of any such penalty.*

In criminal cases, a witness, other than the defendant, may claim the privilege in the circumstances set out in s. 3 of the Evidence Act (1851) which provides:

> *But nothing herein contained shall render any person who in any criminal proceeding is charged with the commission of any indictable offence, or any offence punishable on summary conviction, competent or compellable to give evidence for against himself or herself, or shall render any person compellable to answer any question tending to criminate himself or herself, or shall in any criminal proceeding render any husband competent or compellable to give evidence for or against his wife, or any wife competent or compellable to give evidence for or against her husband.*

The privilege applies in all courts, tribunals, inquiries and other similar proceedings, so that even a Parliamentary sub-committee cannot compel a witness to answer a question if to do so would tend to incriminate him.

However, once the risk of prosecution ceases, so does the right to claim the privilege, so that where proceedings for a particular offence must be commenced within a fixed time, once that time has expired the witness can no longer sustain the claim on the basis of a risk of prosecution for that offence notwithstanding the fact that he may have done so earlier.

ENTRAPMENT

There may be other objections to admissibility, particularly in criminal proceedings, such as where tape-recordings are deliberately made to entrap the employee. The issue of entrapment does not apply to internal disciplinary hearings or to Employment Tribunals.

Entrapment is a legal term of art which, in its purest sense, means the inducement, by a police officer or a police agent, of the commission of an offence which the defendant would not otherwise have committed.

DETECTING POTENTIAL BREACH OF CONTRACT – GOING TO WORK FOR A COMPETITOR

Where the prime aim of the monitoring is the detection of competitive activity, informing the employees will usually be counterproductive. Knowing that they are being monitored, the majority of employees will simply make and receive their telephone calls elsewhere.

Similarly where there are restrictive covenants including non-compete clauses and the employer has suspicions that the employee in question is preparing to leave or has given notice to resign to go to work for a competitor, the employer may wish to monitor their telephone calls.

Several years ago, a hospital authority had grounds to suspect a consultant had taken bribes in relation to the placing of an extremely valuable contract for medical equipment. The hospital management authorised secret recording of his telephones in order to try to detect this wrongdoing and succeeded.

HUMAN RIGHTS

In the light of the Human Rights Act 1998, which came into force in England and Wales on 2 October 2000, the Office of Telecommunications (OFTEL) published (on 19 August 1999) guidance on recording telephone calls which states that employees must be able to make *personal* calls that are not recorded. Employers who do not provide this guarantee of confidentiality could be in breach of the European Convention on Human Rights, art. 8 which establishes the right to respect for private life.

In the case of *Halford* v *United Kingdom* [1997] IRLR 471, the European Court of Human Rights considered the application of Article 8(1) in the context of a case involving surveillance by an employer of an employee's office telephone.

The court held that, since the employee had not been given any prior warning that her telephone calls were liable to interception by her employer, she had a reasonable expectation of privacy for such calls.

The court therefore concluded that the telephone calls were covered by Article 8 and that the interception by the employer of those calls was an unlawful breach of that article. In her case her calls on a private line to her lawyers were recorded by her employers during the course of her sex discrimination litigation against them.

The same reasoning applies in relation to the interception of other forms of electronic communications, including email and the internet.

REASONABLE EXPECTATION OF PRIVACY

It would appear from the Halford decision that if an employee does not have a reasonable expectation of privacy, then an employer may be free to intercept communications. However, if as in the case of Alison Halford, an employee has a private telephone line that dials out without going through the switchboard, then they may have a reasonable expectation of privacy on that line.

PERSONAL CALLS – TELEPHONE POLICY

There are a range of policies on the use of the company telephone from absolute prohibition to permission to use the employer's telephones without restriction. These are referred to in more detail in Chapter 11.

Many employers use words such as 'reasonable' and 'occasional' use for private use without charge. This often leads to a debate as to what is 'reasonable' or 'occasional'.

Other employers give guidance such as personal calls should only be made on the company telephones for 'urgent domestic crises'. For other personal telephone calls, public payphones are sometimes provided or personal charge cards can be used to make personal calls on the employer's landlines.

Sometimes the advice refers to making non-urgent personal calls 'only' during 'scheduled breaks or outside normal working hours' when they do not interfere with work requirements.

Employers often limit incoming personal calls to 'domestic crises and arrangements' and employees are exhorted to keep them short.

Where any abuse or misuse of telephones arises, employers will reserve the right to monitor the destination and length of outgoing calls and the source and length of incoming calls. Rarely would this include surveillance, that is, listening in or recording but as one employer puts it 'in rare cases where there are reasonable grounds to suspect gross misconduct, [the employer] reserves the right to record calls'.

In most cases only designated and trained staff are permitted to record calls or receive print-outs of calls and a senior manager only is authorised to grant permission for such recording to take place.

Employees are often asked to report any misuse of company facilities, in the first instance, to Human Resources.

In other cases, such as in the Civil Service, there are special rules about making confidential telephone calls, for example, the mandatory use of secure telephone lines when making or receiving confidential telephone calls.

Often the department head or line manager is left with the difficult decision of determining what is 'excessive' use and what is use 'within reason'.

In some cases employers reserve the right to deduct from salary any telephone calls made overseas or made 'to excess'. Some employers define this as more than two personal calls per day.

A typical clause reads:

> You agree that the Company may deduct from your salary/ wages the cost of personal calls made abroad or made in excess of what your line manager deems reasonable or occasional. This sum may be made as a lump sum from the next payroll following discussion with you concerning this call/these calls. Management may agree to deduct the sums, in tranches, from the following months' salary if to repay the entire amount in one go would cause financial difficulties.
> If in doubt about whether any particular call would be permissible, please ask your line manager first.

OFTEL'S GUIDANCE

OFTEL's guidance published in 1999 stated that companies and organizations that routinely record telephone calls must ensure that their employees are able to make personal calls that are not also recorded under the same system.

OFTEL (now OFCOM) recommended that staff should also be made aware that personal conversations could be recorded on their telephone and should have access to a separate telephone on the premises where they could make and receive personal calls that were not recorded and which could be taken in private.

Companies were warned that if they do not provide this guarantee of confidentiality they could be in breach of Article 8 of the Europe Convention on Human Rights which covers people's right to respect for privacy.

RARE CASES OF SECRET TELEPHONE MONITORING

In rare cases secret telephone recording has been sanctioned by the courts, particularly where to tell the individual beforehand would override the legitimate purpose for the secret recording.

In *R* v *John Paul Allen, Michael Bunting and Mohammed Noor Boodhoo* [2001] Crim LR 739, the Court of Appeal dismissed the three convicted prisoners' appeal that a prison telephone system that was monitored and controlled was not an abuse of the then s.1 of the Interception of Communications Act 1985 or the Telecommunications Act 1984 as the prison service had such a level of control over the prison telephone network that it could not be held to be part of a public telecommunications system.

In this case it was held to be justified that the prison authorities had recorded telephone calls in any event, between the defendants, providing incontrovertible evidence of conspiracy to pervert the course of justice. The third defendant had been a juror who had accepted money to return untrue verdicts.

In *R* v *Ashworth Special Hospital Authority and Secretary of State for Health ex parte N* [2001] LTL 26 June 2001, the High Court held that the Ashworth had not breached Article 8 the right to respect to privacy when they monitored on a random basis the telephone calls of patients in the high security hospital as *'it went no further than was strictly necessary to achieve the permitted aim'*.

The aim was set out in s.4 of the National Health Service Act 1977 which provides that the Secretary of State must *'provide hospital services and accommodation for people detailed under the Mental Health Act 1983 and in his opinion require treatment under conditions of high security on account of their dangerous, violent or criminal propensities'*.

Here, a risk assessment had indicated that it was necessary to carry out random monitoring of patients' telephone calls both incoming and outgoing but this did not include any calls made from or to their lawyers.

OFTEL - GUIDANCE ON RECORDING OF TELEPHONE CONVERSATIONS, REF: 47/99

Date: 19 August 1999

At the request of the Home Office, OFTEL has today published new guidance to companies covering their responsibilities over recording phone calls for business purposes.

Companies and organisations that routinely record telephone calls must ensure that their employees are able to make personal calls that are not also recorded under the same system.

Staff must also be made aware that personal conversations could be recorded on their telephone and must have access to a separate telephone on the premises where they can make and receive personal calls that are not recorded.

Companies that do not provide this guarantee of confidentiality could be in breach of Article 8 of the Europe Convention on Human Rights which covers people's right to privacy.

This new OFTEL publication intended to help Companies in the private sector follows a recent Home Office circular issued to all public bodies on this matter. OFTEL has agreed separately to publicise this issue to other organisations.

NOTE TO EDITORS

The Home Office circular was issued in response to the European Court of Human Rights (ECtHR) decision in June 1997 on the case of Halford vs UK. The essence of the judgement was that interception of a person's office telephone can constitute an interference with the right to respect for their private life established under Article 8 ECHR. Where this is so, the interception must be carried out in accordance with the law and there must be an effective remedy. Because UK law relating to interception does not currently extend to non-public telephone networks, this form of interception could not be carried out in accordance with the law and consequently there was no effective remedy.

RECORDING TELEPHONE CONVERSATIONS ON PRIVATE NETWORKS

This note contains new advice to companies that provide telephone services to their employees. This is published at the request of the Home Office who wish to alert such companies to a new and important legal interpretation of their obligations concerning the privacy of their employees' telephone calls.

This advice is necessary to ensure that the UK is compliant with the European Convention on Human Rights (ECHR) and a recent ruling in the European Court of Human Rights (ECtHR). If you run a company or are in any way responsible within your company or organisation for the provision of telephone services, you need to read, understand and act on this new advice. This includes any organisation that runs its own switchboard, call centre or other type of private voice network.

The present position

Several factors have contributed to the growing practice of recording or monitoring telephone conversations at the work place in recent years. Within the financial services sector it has become widely accepted even where it is not strictly a regulatory requirement. The growth of call centres has led to a significant expansion in the amount of business done by telephone. The need to ensure customer satisfaction, to train and supervise call centre staff, to achieve quality targets, to have a record of what was said in the event of a subsequent dispute – all these have inevitably led to widespread monitoring and recording of calls.

Where organisations do feel it necessary to record or monitor calls – for whatever reasons – the rules under which they do so have been set by the Privacy of Messages condition of the major two telecoms class licences – the Self-Provision (SPL) and Telecommunication Services (TSL) Licences. The most fundamental requirement of this condition has been that every reasonable effort is made to inform all parties to a telephone conversation that it may or will be recorded. Annex 1 provides an extract of the relevant section of the SPL/TSL.

Although the condition does not specify precisely how the parties should be informed, most people will now be aware of how many firms are conforming to the requirement. Advertisements that invite calls to a given number, whether the advert appears as a poster, on television or radio or in the print media, frequently carry a message to the effect that calls may be recorded or monitored for quality.

Why new guidance now?

Effective as the SPL/TSL rules have been they were not designed to address the broader legal issues, pertaining to privacy, that can arise with recording and monitoring. These rules effectively regulate how an organisation should give relevant parties warning about recording or monitoring, but do not fully elaborate the privacy rights of employees in the workplace. The new advice, based on the ECtHR judgement, focuses on the reasonable expectation of privacy that employees are entitled to in the workplace – an entitlement conferred by the European Convention on Human Rights that is going to be incorporated into UK law by the Human Rights Act 1998.

The purpose of the new Home Office guidance is to clarify what employers need to do now, in advance of proposed legislative changes, to comply with the Convention and the lessons learned from the judgement.

Under the new advice, the present SPL/TSL rules remain valid, but the new Home Office advice is based upon the principle that "everyone has the right to respect for his private and family life, his home and his correspondence" established by the European Convention on Human Rights. It may not therefore be sufficient simply to warn employees that their phone calls at work may be recorded or monitored in order to remove their expectation of privacy. This is because it is not reasonable to assume that people at work will never make or receive calls touching on personal and domestic matters. One lesson to be drawn from the judgement is that there is a legitimate expectation of privacy for such calls.

This means that there has to be some way in which employees at work can make or receive personal calls that will not be recorded or monitored. The circular suggests that one way of doing this would be for an employer to provide adequate access to payphones in the workplace with an undertaking that they will not be subject to any form of recording or monitoring. However this is not the only way of meeting this objective. The key issue is that there are some lines at work which members of staff can use for private calls secure in the confidence that calls made from them will not be recorded or monitored.

It is equally important that employees continue to be informed that recording or monitoring may take place on official work phones, as already required by the SPL/TSL. The main reason for this is that once there has been a clear explanation that calls made on a particular system may be recorded or monitored, anyone making calls on that system is acknowledging the possibility that those calls may be recorded or monitored. This can be interpreted as implied consent and removes the expectation of privacy. As OFTEL has previously advised, the necessary information can be given within a work environment in a number of ways including terms and conditions of employment, staff notices, posters and global e-mails.

External callers also need to be advised of the possibility of recording or monitoring. Companies have devised a number of appropriate ways to meet this requirement, including the use warnings in advertising and customer literature.

What else should be done?

Although it may not be a strict legal necessity, it is certainly good practice to explain to staff why their calls might be recorded or monitored. Moreover this will offer a higher degree of protection in the case of a legal challenge. Employers should develop guidelines covering their policy on recording and monitoring in the workplace and the use they will make of the material derived from it.

It is however advisable to restrict recording and monitoring activities to situations where they are both absolutely necessary and proportionate to the problem to be overcome. For example, misuse of office phones could be detected by an itemised call record, which is less intrusive than recording or monitoring of the actual calls.

Conclusion

In conclusion, the main lessons to be drawn are that employees in the workplace are entitled to privacy for any personal calls they may make; that their expectation of privacy for work-related calls must be removed by adequate warning and that where their privacy is affected it must be for some purpose which is both reasonable and proportionate.

THE PRIVACY OF MESSAGES CONDITION OF THE SELF-PROVISION LICENCE (SPL) AND THE TELECOMMUNICATION SERVICES LICENCE (TSL).

(7.1) The Licensee shall not use or allow to be used any Apparatus comprised in or connected to the Applicable Systems (except for Apparatus connected to or comprised in the Applicable Systems for the purpose of law enforcement or in the interest of national security) which is capable of recording, silently monitoring (except for monitoring where the meaningful content of the Message is not monitored) or intruding into Live Speech Telephone Calls, unless he complies with paragraphs 7.3 and 7.4. This paragraph shall not apply if the Licensee is an Emergency Organisation or if the Director has consented to the Licensee not complying with any or all of paragraphs 7.3 and 7.4 and has not withdrawn that consent.

(7.2) The provisions of each consent given under paragraph 7.1 shall be entered in the register kept by the Director for the purpose of section 19 of the Act.

(7.3) The Licensee shall make every reasonable effort to inform parties to whom or by whom a Live Speech Telephone Call is transmitted before recording, silent monitoring or intrusion into such Call has begun that the Live Speech Telephone Call is to be or may be recorded, silently monitored or intruded into.

(7.4) The Licensee shall maintain a record of the means by which parties to whom or by whom a Live Speech Telephone Call is transmitted have been informed that such Call is to be or may be recorded, silently monitored or intruded into. The Licensee shall furnish to the Director such information on request.

CHAPTER 4

Disciplining and Dismissing Employees

RULES MUST BE CLEAR

Employers are entitled to establish the rules about the use and misuse of the company internet, telephone, postal service and email system.

The one important feature of any set of rules is the clarity of those rules and the consequences for breach of those rules. In other words the rules must be in writing, must have been given to all employees, must be reviewed and promulgated at regular intervals and must be clear as to which category of employee could be dismissed for a single first offence.

It is possible for employers to distinguish between different categories of employee making it more or less serious to abuse or misuse the email/internet as long as those employees who may be dismissed for a single, first, important breach of the rules are fully aware of the consequences and what they are forbidden from doing.

The importance of clearly-defined disciplinary rules was stressed by the Employment Appeal Tribunal (EAT) in *Dairy Produce Packers Ltd* v *Beverstock* [1981] IRLR 265. Here the employer was found to have acted unfairly in dismissing an employee for drinking in a public house during working hours.

The company argued that drinking during working hours outside the factory is more serious than drinking on factory premises and that this justified dismissing Mr Beverstock where others guilty of drinking offences had not been dismissed.

The EAT points out that it is within the employer's discretion to impose differing rules with regard to consumption of alcohol. But if he wishes to do so, this must be clearly laid down and made a term of the contract of employment.

EMPLOYER'S DECISION TO DISMISS MUST BE 'REASONABLE'

A decision to dismiss must be 'reasonable' in accordance with the words of s.98(4) of the Employment Rights Act 1996. This states that an employer must act reasonably in treating *that* reason as sufficient reason for dismissal taking into account all the circumstances of the case including the size and administrative resources of the undertaking and taking into account equity and the substantial merits of the case.

In *Post Office* v *Foley/HSBC Bank* v *Madden* [2000] IRLR 827 the Court of Appeal reviewed the test of reasonableness under s.98(4) of the Employment Rights Act 1996 as amended and confirmed that the test of reasonableness was objective, that is, *Did what this employer do, fall within the band of reasonable responses that any reasonable employer would have adopted?*

It is not for the tribunal to substitute its views for that of the employer.

What the Court of Appeal did in these two conjoined appeals was;

> *to confirm the orthodox approach that a tribunal is not allowed to substitute its own view of what is reasonable for that of the employer. It also, as expected, re-establishes that the obligation to carry out a reasonable investigation in accordance with the test laid down in British Home Stores v Burchell [1978] IRLR 379 is an aspect of reasonableness rather than an issue forming part of the proof of the reason for dismissal as held in Madden [2000] IRLR 288.*

Lord Justice Mummery went on to explain that:

> *The range of reasonable responses approach ... is not required in every case. There will be cases in which there is no band or range to consider. If, for example, an employee, without good cause, deliberately sets fire to his employer's factory and it is burnt to the ground, dismissal is the only reasonable response. If an employee is dismissed for politely saying 'Good morning' to his line manager, that would be an unreasonable response. But in between those extreme cases there will be cases where there is room for reasonable disagreement among reasonable employers as to whether dismissal for the particular misconduct is a reasonable or an unreasonable response. In those cases it is helpful for the tribunal to consider 'the range of reasonable responses.*

All three elements of the test laid down in *British Home Stores* v *Burchell* [1978] IRLR 379 have to be satisfied, as follows:

- Does the employer hold a genuine belief in this reason for dismissal?
- Does the employer have reasonable grounds in his mind in order to sustain that belief? and

- Has the employer carried out as proper and as thorough an investigation into the matter as was reasonable in all the circumstances of the case?

THE PUNISHMENT MUST FIT THE CRIME

Even where employers have made the rules crystal clear, the employer must still go on to demonstrate that in this particular case it was reasonable to dismiss the employee.

So where there is no dishonesty, pre-meditation, deceit, cover-up, no pecuniary advantage to the employee or a mere technical breach of the rules, employers may be found to have unfairly dismissed the employee if they have applied the rule that summary dismissal for a first offence is always the penalty.

In *Ladbroke Racing* v *Arnott and another* [1983] IRLR 154 and *Beckett* v *BBC* [1983] IRLR 43, the Courts held that the 'punishment must fit the crime' and 'the penalty must fall within the ranges of penalties that any reasonable employer could have adopted'.

In *Arnott's* case Mrs Arnott and Mrs Paris both long-serving and with hitherto unblemished records had placed several 50p bets at their place of work in breach of a clear instruction, notice and term of their contract that they were not allowed to do so. It had always been done in front of their supervisor who was aware of what they had done on every occasion. Both women owned up immediately when asked whether they had placed the bets and both had done so on behalf of other individuals and not for any pecuniary gain to themselves. The Court of Session dismissed the employer's appeal that the rule was clear – no-one working at Ladbrokes was permitted to place a bet on their own behalf or on behalf of anyone else and the rule went on to say that anyone who was found to have breached the rule would face 'instant dismissal'.

The Court of Session ruled that:

> *The standard of acting reasonably set by s.57(3) (now s. 98(4)) requires an employer to consider all the facts relevant to the nature and cause of the breach, including the degree of its gravity. If, therefore, the employer has a rule prohibiting a specific act for which the stated penalty is instant dismissal, he does not satisfy s.57(3) by imposing that penalty without regard to any facts or circumstances other than the breach itself. If that was a legitimate approach, it would follow that any breach of rules so framed would constitute gross misconduct warranting dismissal irrespective of the manner in which the breach occurred.*

> *In the present case, there was nothing to indicate that the manager who took the decision to dismiss the respondents gave any thought to the provisions of s.57(3) by considering whether the nature of the admitted breaches was such that in all the circumstances the breaches warranted dismissal. Matters that should have been taken into account were that the conduct in question involved relatively minor infringements of the rule; that there was no personal advantage to the respondents; that the respondents were under the impression that what they were doing was sanctioned by a superior officer; and that the breaches of the rule only came to light because of the respondents' own admissions. The appeal would be dismissed.*

In *Beckett's* case the employer attempted to downgrade him – a penalty provided for in the disciplinary procedure. However the EAT held that 'the imposition of a punishment was "grossly out of proportion to the offence"'. Here Mr Beckett was an outside broadcast carpenter who had left for lunch leaving a small rostrum unsafe. He was downgraded to work in the BBC premises thus causing him a large loss of privileges and perks. He resigned and claimed constructive dismissal arguing that the imposition of such a penalty was grossly disproportionate to the offence that he had committed.

NEW PROCEDURE

Under the Employment Act 2002, Schedule 2 and the Employment Act 2002 (Dispute Resolution) Regulations 2004, employers must follow the minimum standard procedure before taking any decision to dismiss.

This procedure involves:

Step 1: statement of grounds for action and invitation to meeting

(1) The employer must set out in writing the employee's alleged conduct or other circumstances, which led the employer to contemplate dismissing or taking disciplinary action against the employee.

(2) The employer must send the statement or a copy of it to the employee and invite the employee to attend a meeting to discuss the matter.

Step 2: meeting

2(1) The meeting must take place before any action is taken or decision is made, except in the case where the disciplinary action consists of suspension.

(2) The meeting must not take place unless:

(a) the employer has informed the employee what the basis was for believing that the employee has committed the offence. This will include copying to the employee in advance all the documentary evidence upon which the employer intends to rely;

(b) the employee has had a reasonable opportunity to consider and prepare his response to that information;

(c) the employer must inform the employee of his rights to be accompanied to the meeting with a fellow worker or trade union representative.

(3) The employee must take all reasonable steps to attend the meeting.

(4) After the meeting, the employer must inform the employee of his decision and notify him of the right to appeal against the decision if he is not satisfied with it.

Step 3: appeal

3(1) If the employee does wish to appeal, he must inform the employer.(2) If the employee informs the employer of his wish to appeal, the employer must invite him to attend a further meeting. The grounds of appeal consist of:

(a) new evidence not available at the time of the original hearing;

(b) too harsh a penalty: or

(c) the original hearing was unfair, biased or prejudiced and the employee was not given any chance to defend himself.

(3) The employee must take all reasonable steps to attend the meeting.

(4) The appeal meeting need not take place before the dismissal or disciplinary action takes effect.

(5) After the appeal meeting, the employer must inform the employee of his final decision.

FACTORS TO TAKE INTO ACCOUNT

The case law suggests that it is essential not to respond to the commission of an offence by operating a tariff approach. Employers are exhorted to take into account the individual circumstances of each case. Culpability, blameworthiness, insight into their wrongdoing, contrition and the employee's attitude during the disciplinary hearing are very important factors.

One Employment Tribunal dismissed the complaint of a long-serving operative who, instead of checking the equipment, remained in his control room reading a magazine. The individual asked the manager holding the disciplinary hearing, whether *he* would have rather walked round the plant checking the equipment or would have rather sat in the control room, reading a magazine, looking up to the plant through a hole in the ceiling (*McKenzie* v *Amylum (UK) Ltd* Case No: 2305765/2003).

In *Paul* v *East Surrey District Health Authority* [1995] IRLR 305 the Court of Appeal held that factors such as the employee showing contrition, insight into what they have done, admits that they have done wrong and shows that they are worthy of being given a second chance, should all be 'weighed' by an employer when determining whether dismissal for a first offence is a reasonable response.

In *Paul's* case following a warning to all nursing staff that no alcohol was to be consumed on duty, Mr Paul and two other charge nurses were found to have been drinking on duty. Mr Paul was dismissed while the other two were reprimanded.

On appeal against his dismissal, Mr Paul maintained that he had been treated differently from other employees who had been found to have been drinking on duty. Particular instances were cited, including the case of Mr Paul's own supervisor, a senior charge nurse, who had been drinking whisky with him on the night in question but who had received only a reprimand and formal warning. Another employee who had admitted her misconduct, said that it was due to personal problems and agreed to undergo counselling, was not dismissed until the third occasion on which she was found to have been drinking on duty.

The Court of Appeal held that:

> *An employer is entitled to take into account not only the nature of the conduct and the surrounding facts but also any mitigating personal circumstances affecting the employee concerned. The attitude of the employee to his conduct may be a relevant factor in deciding whether a repetition is likely. Thus an employee who admits that the conduct proved is unacceptable and accepts advice and help to avoid a repetition may be regarded differently from one who refuses to accept responsibility for his actions, argues with management or makes unfounded suggestions that his fellow employees have conspired to accuse him falsely.*

In *Securicor Ltd* v *Smith* [1989] IRLR 356 the Court of Appeal held that:

> *The question for the Industrial Tribunal was whether or not the employers acted reasonably and within the band of reasonable responses in acting upon the findings and conclusions of the appeal panel.*
>
> *Therefore, where two employees are dismissed for the same incident and one is successful on appeal but the other is not, in determining the fairness of the latter's dismissal the question is whether the appeal panel's decision was so irrational that no employer could reasonably have accepted it.*
>
> *In the present case, the employers had not acted unreasonably in accepting the appeal panel's decision that the respondent was more culpable for the incident. The appeal panel distinguished between the culpability of the two employees on the basis of causation and decided that the respondent's appeal should be dismissed but that of the other employee allowed.*
>
> *... Although it would have been open to the appeal panel to reach a different conclusion, they did not do so for rational and clear reasons.*

THE RULES

The rules about use and misuse of the internet and email range from absolute prohibition to use at the discretion of the employee. In between some employers allow for private use of internet and email at work before the official start time and after normal office hours and during breaks.

Employers who seek to ban any private use of the email or internet will need to set out the rules very clearly explaining the reasons, for example, abuse of work time; possibility of excessive time spent not working; possibility of unsuitable material being distributed or downloaded; possibility of disrepute being caused to employer.

MAKING STAFF AWARE OF THE RULES

Time and time again employers lose at tribunal because they have not sufficient evidence to show that they have brought the rules to the attention of their staff and most importantly emphasized what kind of conduct can lead to summary dismissal even for a first offence.

In *Dunn* v *IBM United Kingdom* Case No: 2305087/97 Mr Dunn's summary dismissal was held to be unfair after he had admitted accessing pornography via the internet and making printouts of downloaded pictures. In this case the tribunal held that it was significant that the employee had admitted the offences without appreciating that the consequence would be his dismissal and the employer had failed to take sufficient steps to advise the staff of the consequences of the abuse of the internet, that is, that it would be treated as gross misconduct and the normal penalty would be summary dismissal.

In *Arnold* v *Merseyside Passenger Transport Executive* (Case No: 2102866/01) the Employment Tribunal found that the dismissal of Mr Arnold was unfair when he was constructively dismissed following the secret monitoring of two private calls to his friends. Mr Arnold had worked for 11 years in the travel information call centre. The Employment Tribunal held that because neither Mr Arnold nor his colleagues had been warned that their telephone calls might be monitored and that private calls were banned, his employers had acted unreasonably in dismissing him for making private telephone calls. In addition because the employer was in the public sector they had breached both the Human Rights Act 1998 and Regulation of Investigatory Powers Act 2000.

In *Crook* v *Manpower Services,* John Crook lost his unfair dismissal claim for sending an email to his boss, recommending a colleague for a pay rise. Crook had praised her work rate and then added: 'And she was a grrrreat shag as well.'

Mr Crook's explanation that he knew his boss well and believed that she would find the remark amusing. Mr Crook argued that the colleague about whom he had written had seen the email and had also thought it funny. The tribunal did not believe him.

In two other cases, both involving firms of solicitors, the mass distribution of personal emails caused huge embarrassment to both employers (see Norton Rose and Baker & McKenzie cases in Chapter 5). In Chapter 11 we will look at a variety of different policies that could afford some protection against this type of conduct.

SLIDING SCALE OF PUNISHMENTS

It may be appropriate to have a sliding scale of offences concerning misuse of the email and internet at work. The more serious the breach of the rule, the more harsh the penalty may be. So downloading or distributing offensive material may warrant a far more harsh penalty than merely wasting time emailing colleagues asking them to put the kettle on!

So for wasting office time writing and receiving private emails on a relatively small scale, a first written warning might be appropriate. A first occasion of accessing a prohibited site such as a gambling site might also evoke a first written warning. In contrast accessing, downloading and/or distributing offensive or pornographic sites or sending offensive messages or attachments by email could be deemed to be gross misconduct for which summary dismissal could be a reasonable penalty.

Depending upon the seriousness of the time wasting and inappropriateness of the sites, the employer would have the right to scale up or down the penalty.

In *Pennington and Beverley* v *Holset Engineering Ltd* Case No: 802184/00 the Leeds Employment Tribunal held that it was fair and reasonable for the employer to draw up a 'rating list' and rank certain employees according to the level of offensiveness and number of emails sent. In this case the employer had made it clear that computers were to be used for work purposes only. Clear warnings had gone out to all staff that computers were only to be used for work purposes and what consequences would follow if misuse of the email/internet occurred. These two individuals had both sent offensive emails on more than one occasion. Although the Employment Tribunal accepted that there was some element of subjectivity, they held that such a system was fair and reasonable.

Even where an employee admits and acknowledges that they have made excessive personal telephone calls, this does not absolve the employer from carrying out a thorough investigation into the matter including interviewing other staff to see whether such conduct was widespread and investigating whether the employer's policy regarding the use of the company telephone for personal use was well known and understood by staff.

In *Johnson* v *Scottish & Newcastle plc (S&N)* EAT 1028/00, Mrs Johnson had been dismissed for making excessive private calls on the pub's telephone when she managed one of S&N's public houses.

She accepted that she had done wrong in the extent of the use of the telephone for her private use. The Employment Tribunal had found that the employers had failed to carry out any form of reasonable investigation (see third limb of *Burchell* test above) as they had not interviewed any other members of staff nor had they had made any enquiry to see how far the company's policy on the use of the telephone was known or understood by staff. Such investigations might have revealed that private calls had been made by some of the other staff.

However, her compensation was reduced by 95% on her basic award and 90% on her compensatory award for contributory fault.

The fact that an employee admits that what they have done is wrong is far from admitting that their dismissal was either reasonable or inevitable.

The EAT held that:

> *Whether the failure to investigate sufficiently, as decided by the Tribunal, may properly be regarded as a procedural or substantive flaw, it cannot be said to be purely marginal or peripheral, as the question whether the telephone use policy was communicated to staff and the extent to which other members of staff may or may not have abused the telephone were plainly capable of having a substantial impact on the nice balance which the Tribunal had to apply in deciding whether the decision to dismiss was within the range of reasonable responses.*

In another case, withdrawn before the hearing, a female member of staff was found to have sent over 285 emails within the space of five days to her boyfriend, a lorry driver, offering and asking for many and varied sexual favours. This only came to light after a customer had alleged that they had not received confirmation by email of the order that they had placed. In checking her email server, the IT Department discovered over 200 personal emails sent by this lady over the space of five days.

She initially denied that there was anything offensive or salacious about the contents of the emails until she was asked whether her husband would be of the same opinion!

SOME EMPLOYEES ARE EXPECTED TO KNOW!

In *Morrison* v *Avocet hardware plc* [2003] ALL ER 126 the Employment Tribunal dealt with an interesting issue relating to monitoring of telephone calls made at work.

In this case, the employer and the employee asserted different human rights in support of their claims. The Employment Appeal Tribunal had to determine which was more important.

Mr Morrison was a telesales operative who, by definition, spent most of his working day on the telephone. Unbeknown to Mr Morrison, his bosses were monitoring his calls. When they took exception to the contents of one of his calls, they dismissed him summarily for gross misconduct.

Mr Morrison claimed unfair dismissal. His employer in defending the claim sought to adduce as evidence the contents of the phone call as justifying its decision.

The tribunal ruled that the evidence was inadmissible, on the basis that because Mr Morrison had been unaware of the monitoring, the way in which the evidence had been obtained infringed his right to respect for his private life under the Human Rights Act.

The employer appealed.

The Employment Appeal Tribunal took the view that it would be unusual for *'those engaged in business on the telephone not to be aware that their talk might be monitored'.*

Although the tribunal accepted the employer's evidence might have been obtained in breach of the Human Rights Act, this did not necessarily lead to the conclusion that it could not be admitted in tribunal proceedings.

The employer, although a plc, 'had human rights too', in this case the right to a fair trial under Article 6. Because the contents of the telephone call were crucial to the employer's justification for dismissal, it had to be admitted into evidence regardless of the method by which it was obtained.

Covert evidence was also admitted by the Scottish Court of Session in *Martin* v *McGuiness* [2003] ScotCS 96 but in this case no order as to costs was made.

In *Robert A McGowan v Scottish Water* [2004] EATS/0007/04, the Employment Appeal Tribunal held that an employee's right to respect for private and family life under the European Convention on Human Rights 1950 Art.8. was not breached by his employer carrying out covert surveillance. On the facts, such surveillance was not disproportionate.

The employee had appealed against a decision of the employment tribunal that he had not been unfairly dismissed by the respondent employer (Scottish Water).

Following suspicions that McGowan had submitted falsified timesheets, Scottish Water had decided to use covert surveillance on McGowan. McGowan was subsequently dismissed in accordance with the employer's disciplinary procedure.

The tribunal determined that the process was fair and that the surveillance had not breached McGowan's right to respect for private and family life under the European Convention on Human Rights 1950 Art.8. McGowan submitted that the tribunal misdirected itself on the issue of Art.8(1) of the Convention and that the surveillance was disproportionate.

The Employment Appeal Tribunal held that Scottish Water was a public corporation investigating what was effectively criminal activity. The surveillance went to the heart of the investigation that the employer was bound to carry out to protect the assets of the company. The surveillance was not undertaken for external or whimsical reasons and was not disproportionate. It had to be borne in mind that the suspicions of Scottish Water were found to be established and that the subsequent disciplinary process resulted in McGowan being dismissed on grounds of dishonesty. The tribunal was entitled to reach the conclusion that Art.8 of the Convention was not breached on the evidence.

It seems that the courts and tribunals are now more likely to allow illegally obtained covert evidence that is directly relevant to legal proceedings than to exclude it. To that extent it would appear that the balance between the right to a fair trial and the individual's right to respect for privacy is tipped in favour of a right to a fair trial.

However, an employee whose rights under the Data Protection Act 1998 or RIPA have been breached may well succeed in a claim for damages. Furthermore in claims for personal injuries, employers who collect illegal covert evidence may be the subject of a costs order even if they win (see *Jones* v *University of Warwick*).

CASES

One of the first reported cases of 'electronic' related misconduct arose in *Denco Ltd* v *Joinson* [1991] IRLR 63. Mr Joinson gained unauthorised access to pay data by watching and memorising the wages supervisor's password. Mr Joinson wanted this pay data for collective bargaining as he was a shop steward.

He was dismissed for gross misconduct. The EAT held that it was critical for employers to have very clear and accessible rules about use and misuse of computerised data:

> *Unauthorised use of, or tampering with, computers is an extremely serious industrial offence. If an employee uses an unauthorised password in order to enter or attempt to enter a computer known to contain information to which he is not entitled, that of itself is gross misconduct which prima facie will attract summary dismissal.*
>
> *The employee's motive is immaterial.*
>
> *It is a question of "absolutes" and should be compared with dishonesty. An analogy may be drawn with a situation where an employee enters the management offices of a company where he has no right to be, goes into an office, sees a key on the desk which he knows is the key to a filing cabinet containing information to which he is not entitled and thereafter opens the cabinet and takes out a file.*

> *It is desirable, however, that management should make it abundantly clear to the workforce that interfering with computers will carry severe penalties. Rules concerning access to and use of computers should be reduced to writing and left near the computers for reference.*

One of the first reported cases on misuse of the internet was that of *Lois Franxhi* v *Focus Management Consultants Ltd* (14 June 1998, Case No 2102862/98). An Employment Tribunal upheld the employer's dismissal for gross misconduct of Mrs Franxhi's use of the internet facility for private purposes. They held that it amounted to flagrant abuse of company property.

Mrs Franxhi was employed as a personal assistant to two directors for a period of three years before her summary dismissal in July 1998.

She was regarded as a 'very trusted employee' in a working environment that relied on 'the minimum of regulation and the maximum of trust'.

A few weeks after being given a written warning for helping herself to company stamps for private post, Mrs Franxhi was accused of abusing the company's internet facility. She was found to have used the internet to arrange her holiday.

The evidence submitted to the tribunal revealed extensive use of the internet over a period of several days. When asked about her use of the internet, Mrs Franxhi lied, claiming to have only used the internet once during her lunch break.

During the disciplinary hearing, Mrs Franxhi said that she had never been told not to make personal telephone calls or use the internet. She therefore did not accept that she had done anything wrong.

Her employer accepted that more effort should have been made to ensure that employees were aware that extensive private use of company property was not allowed.

Following a hearing, she was summarily dismissed on grounds of misconduct. She complained to an Employment Tribunal that she had been dismissed for being pregnant, which she argued was an inadmissible reason for dismissal, a breach of contract and sex discrimination. The tribunal disagreed.

The Tribunal held that:

> *[As] a senior employee, she must have known that the extensive private use of the Internet was not allowed, any more than any other extensive private use of a company asset was'.*

A printed record of Mrs Franxhi's use of the internet was submitted to the tribunal evidencing the extent of her internet usage. This record substantiated the respondent's genuine belief in Mrs Franxhi's abuse of the internet facility.

The tribunal held that:

> *Her use of the Internet was more than the occasional fleeting one that might conceivably have been regarded as open to everyone. She used it wholesale and spent a long time on it. She must have known that such use was not acceptable to the employer.*

In order to avoid confusion, employers should ensure that an email policy is properly drawn up and communicated to all employees specifying boundaries for use of this type of company property.

When assessing employee use of the internet, companies should consider implementing methods for monitoring its use. These may be covered in the email policy and should include provision for notifying the employees of any monitoring/surveillance with or without their prior knowledge. The existence of a policy demonstrates that an employer has taken reasonable care to prevent abuse and misuse of any internet or email facilities accessible to employees.

If employees are warned about conduct that is considered unacceptable which may lead to summary dismissal, employers will find it easier to persuade a tribunal that it has acted reasonably in deciding to dismiss.

In another case - *Humphries* v *VH Barnett & Co*, it was held that:

> *the mere use of the Internet for unauthorised purposes would not ordinarily justify summary dismissal unless such conduct was expressly described as gross misconduct in the employer's policies.*

This case illustrates that the mere fact that an employer makes a rule that there should be no private use of the email or internet cannot automatically render the dismissal of an employee for a breach of that rule, fair.

The treatment of others is also relevant and likely to be important evidence in any Tribunal claim. In *D McLuskey* v *Duty and Tax Free World International Ltd* EAT/1369/00 the EAT allowed an appeal against a strike out of the claimant's case where his witness statement contained irrelevant allegations and in so doing stated:

> *It is no surprise that an issue in this case became that other members of staff of the employers were also sending lewd and pornographic emails to each other. We say this because it is a natural consequence*

of an assertion that the dismissal is not within the band of reasonable responses. One only has to posit the position of a company in which nobody sends these types of e-mail one to another and ask whether e-mails containing the language particularised by the employers would, or would not, warrant immediate dismissal to recognise that a defence may be "Well I was sending those e-mails but so was everybody else."

In *Morse* v *Future Reality Ltd* Case No: 54571/95 *London North Employment Tribunal,* the female applicant was obliged to share an office with several men who allegedly spent a considerable amount of their time studying sexually explicit images downloaded from the internet. It was not suggested that these activities were directed at the applicant personally but understandably they caused her embarrassment and discomfort. Eventually she resigned and made a claim of sex discrimination based on harassment. As well as the pictures the applicant claimed that bad language was used and that there was a general atmosphere of obscenity in the office. The complaint was upheld principally on the basis that no action had been taken to prevent the behaviour complained of. The applicant was awarded three months' lost earnings and £750 for injury to feelings.

Finally, a Barclaycard employee lost his claim for unfair dismissal after being dismissed for sending insulting emails to other members of staff and commercially sensitive emails to a competitor. Hilary Miseroy had worked in the fraud prevention department for over 15 years. Following the distribution of offensive jokes to other members of staff, the Firm launched an investigation into his email 'Sent Box' and discovered 900 personal emails including messages of a highly derogatory and offensive nature about colleagues. These included referring to one female colleague as having 'a face like a crimewatch victim' and asking another woman if she 'was up for it'. Barclaycard was able to demonstrate that it had a strict email policy about which staff were reminded at regular intervals.

LOG-ON MESSAGES

Some employers have log-on messages that appear when an employee logs on to the email and/or internet:

> **Remember!**
>
> The misuse of the email and internet across the Group is regarded as a serious breach of the Company's data protection policy and equal opportunities policy. The Group takes all misuse of its property and data protection and its equal opportunities policies very seriously and abuse of the system will result in serious disciplinary action including summary dismissal.
>
> In particular, the accessing, downloading, distribution and viewing of illegal games, pornographic and/or other offensive material from the Internet or the sending, viewing or distributing of offensive emails, whether in the form of pictures or words is regarded as gross misconduct and could lead to summary dismissal.
>
> Files including emails sent and received will be periodically reviewed by the Company, without warning, for non-business material and disciplinary action will be taken against anyone who breaches these rules.
>
> **SO PLEASE DON'T DO IT !**

CHAPTER 5

Harassment, Diversity and Pornography

INTRODUCTION

Cases that have hit the headlines are inevitably the ones that contain salacious and intimate sexual details showing staff and sometimes senior management and even solicitors surfing the web, accessing pornographic material and distributing the material to other colleagues both internally and to other organizations.

According to a survey administered by the Chartered Institute of Personnel and Development (CIPD) in 2002, most internet abuse dismissals related to porn and one in four employers surveyed had dismissed some workers for internet misuse, out of which 69 per cent related to pornography.

A more recent survey, in June 2005, from the Audit Commission, found that more men admit to viewing pornography at work than women but a greater proportion of women who visit porn sites claim to do so intentionally.

The report states that downloading porn at work now represents nearly 50 per cent of all IT abuse cases. Some 72 per cent of firms reported that they have dealt with internet misuse in their workplace, and a further 69 per cent of all such dismissals were related to employees visiting porn sites. The report found that 23 per cent of men admit to viewing porn at work, compared to 12 per cent of women, but 11 per cent of women said they visited the sites intentionally, compared to 17 per cent of men.

Seventy per cent of all internet porn traffic, according to the Audit Commission's poll, occurs during the 9 to 5 workday.

Employers must be able to distinguish between someone who seeks to find illegal material and someone who inadvertently clicks on an email link. This can easily be done by examining the internet history files to see whether a webpage was accessed or whether a 'gif' file or 'image' was downloaded as a result of a banner or in-lining.

DISMISSAL OF CHIEF EXECUTIVE

Even chief executives of well-known companies are not protected from dismissal when they indulge in objectionable internet practices. In 2004, Mike Soden, the Chief Executive of the Bank of Ireland, resigned during the course of an audit into his internet activities. The results of the audit revealed that he had accessed an adult website on 2 April 2004, which advertised call girls in the Las Vegas region. The site contained pictures of many of the women advertising their services. This was contrary to the Bank's rules about not accessing inappropriate sites.

AMNESTY GIVEN AT THE FORD MOTOR COMPANY

In March 2004, workers at car manufacturers Ford UK were given two weeks to clear internet porn from their computers. This clampdown by Ford was outlined in an email sent to their 20 000 workers.

OTHER DISMISSALS

There have been multiple instances of employees being sacked for accessing or distributing porn, ranging from the mobile phone network operator, Orange, to stockbrokers and investment bankers, Merrill Lynch, who sacked 15 members of its London staff for sending offensive material from its system.

Civil servants are not exempt from such misconduct. Over 1000 civil servants were caught in 2004 accessing banned websites or abusing emails. In Northern Ireland 332 civil servants were caught infringing the internet and email rules with 219 found to have viewed offensive material.

The Inland Revenue also disciplined 332 staff, half of them for unauthorised access to websites. On 26 August 2004, the Department for Work and Pensions (DWP) dismissed 16 employees and disciplined 227 others who had accessed internet porn at work. The DWP had begun investigating internet abuse in December 2003.

Over two million pornographic web pages had been accessed by DWP civil servants in the eight months since the investigation began. According to a newspaper report, one civil servant had since been convicted for downloading child porn and the police were investigating two others.

The DWP regularly screened its computers for potentially offensive and inappropriate material and it revealed that in the majority of cases where monitoring had picked up apparent inappropriate use, further investigation showed that staff innocently followed a link from another site and were unaware of its content.

DISTRIBUTING AND FORWARDING EMAILS

In the case of *Coleman* v 1) *Lansdowne Capital Ltd* and 2) *Alan Dargan* Case Nos:2204067/2001 and 2204067/2001 emails from Herbert Smith, City Solicitors, were found in the claimant's email 'Saved' messages box, on the company's server which contained the words of a sexually explicit song and 'rude' jokes.

The sexually explicit emails sent on 7 December 2000 by Claire Swire to her boyfriend Bradley Chait who worked at Norton Rose, solicitors, which was forwarded to many thousands of people, demonstrates the power and efficiency of the email service. This email chain was forwarded by Mr Chait to some of his work colleagues as Ms Swire had described their love-making in highly complimentary terms. One of Mr Chait's colleagues emailed the following message *'beggars belief. I feel honour bound to circulate this'* and the rest, as they say, is history.

This one email was forwarded round the globe and was estimated to have been read by over one million people.

BANNING INAPPROPRIATE MATERIAL IN THE WORKPLACE

The Sex Discrimination Act 1975 requires that discrimination occurs where a woman (or a man) is subjected to 'differential', that is, less favourable treatment. However, to prove sex discrimination the woman (or man) has to show, that the comparator (male or female) must be such that the relevant circumstances in the one case are the same or not materially different in the other.

New regulations introduced on 1 October 2005, the Employment Equality (Sex Discrimination) Regulations 2005, introduced a new definition of harassment. Under the new definition a woman no longer has to prove that she has been subjected to detrimental treatment on the grounds of sex. This new right then is supposed to be free-standing. In other words, there is no need for a woman to make a comparison with a male in the same situation as her. If she is upset or humiliated or distressed by the sexist or sexually offensive material, conduct or words, then that should be sufficient to show sexual harassment. Nor conversely should there now be any defence for an employer to say that a man was or would have been treated exactly the same, that is, he was subjected to the sexually offensive pictures or emails and he was not upset or harassed.

The new section 4A of the Sex Discrimination Act 1975 defines harassment including sexual harassment in terms of a person subjecting a woman to harassment, on the grounds of her sex, where a woman's dignity is violated or there is an intimidating, degrading, humiliating or offensive environment.

This can take the form of unwanted verbal, non-verbal physical conduct of a sexual nature that has the purpose of violating her dignity or creating an intimidating, hostile, degrading, humiliating or offensive environment for her, or she is treated less favourably because she has rejected or not submitted to such conduct. Such conduct has to be reasonably viewed as intimidating, hostile, degrading and so on, but the woman's personal perception shall be taken into account. The same applies to the harassment of men.

This should overcome the case law where the employer has been able to argue that pornographic pictures and images placed in the workplace cannot amount to discrimination of women, even if it is only the women who find these images sexually disturbing because they have not been subjected to *differential* treatment. The men have also been subjected to the *same* treatment!

Downloading, viewing and distributing pornographic material will inevitably be regarded as a dismissible offence and as an act of sexual harassment since in most cases women will be offended and intimidated by such material.

Employers should give examples of offensive conduct and should remind staff that any unacceptable conduct of a sexually or racially offensive nature will constitute gross misconduct. In one case, a 'very sick male' cut off the head of a photograph of the young daughter of a male colleague and stuck it onto a sexually disgusting photograph displaying a couple having sexual intercourse. The perpetrator was summarily dismissed for gross misconduct despite the fact that he had not contravened one of the explicit examples of sexually offensive conduct listed in the disciplinary rules.

The decision in *Driskel* v *Peninsula Business Services Ltd* [2000] IRLR 151 was a rare case, prior to the introduction of the regulations, where the Employment Appeal Tribunal sought to interpret the existing Sex Discrimination Act 1975 in a purposive manner. The EAT answered the conundrum, 'How can the same treatment of women and men be less favourable treatment of women than men'?

Here a consultant had complained that her department head had subjected her to a series of sexual comments, culminating in a remark the day before interviewing her for a promotion that she should wear a short skirt and see-through blouse showing plenty of cleavage if she wanted to be successful.

In allowing the appeal, Mr Justice Holland points out that in determining whether sexual banter amounts to sex discrimination, a tribunal should not lose sight of the significance in this context of the sex of both the complainant and the alleged discriminator.

> *Sexual badinage of a heterosexual male by another such cannot be completely equated with like badinage by him of a woman. Prima facie the treatment is not equal: in the latter circumstance it is the sex of the alleged discriminator that potentially adds a material element absent as between two heterosexual men.*

In this case, the employment tribunal erred by putting any weight on the department head's sexual vulgarity towards male employees, since that which he said to men was vulgar without being intimidatory.

RULES AND DISCIPLINARY OFFENCES

Clear rules should be laid down in relation to what materials, photos, magazines, images and so on, are permitted and not permitted at work.

Even the word 'pornographic' means different things to different people.

Literally, pornography means writing about the porne – Greek for a female slave or, in some contexts, a prostitute. Regardless of the means by which it is communicated, pornography has also always been: 'that which exploits and dehumanises sex, so that human beings are treated as things and women in particular as sex objects'.

The *Cambridge Dictionary* definition of pornography is 'books, magazines, films, etc. with no artistic value, which describe or show sexual acts or naked people in a way that is intended to be sexually exciting but would be considered unpleasant or offensive by many people'.

However in one Employment Tribunal claim (which was settled part way through the hearing), the female complainant had alleged that one of the Russian (male) traders had been in the habit of bringing into work pornographic magazines and distributing them to the other traders on her desk.

When questioned about the allegation, that he would open his briefcase in the morning and pull out pornographic magazines, he denied such conduct. In order to 'prove' his innocence, he asked whether he could display the contents of his briefcase. He then produced copies of *Playboy*. When asked whether that was the offensive material to which the complainant had referred, he (and several of his colleagues) retorted that they did not regard *Playboy* as pornography. Their response was that these magazines are displayed and can be purchased on the shelves in WH Smith.

The rules must make it clear that 'any sexually explicit images or text whether this includes nudity or partial nudity which cause or are likely to cause offence to any reasonable person and in particular to a member of the other sex' will fall within the definition of inappropriate material and is banned, whether this can be purchased from the highest or lowest shelf in WH Smith.

GRADING THE OFFENCES AND THE PENALTIES

As we saw in Chapter 4, it is possible to 'grade' the offences into minor, more serious and very serious categories of pornographic or offensive material or conduct. In the first category, employers could categorise 'cyberskiving' or 'wasting time surfing the net' to a limited degree as misconduct warranting either an oral or first written warning for a first offence.

A second category of offence would involve more than an insignificant amount of time spent surfing the web for personal use or the sending and receiving of a more significant number of emails in any given day, which could warrant a final written warning. This would be warranted on the grounds of the amount of time spent surfing the net for personal use or the failure to complete work tasks because of the time spent on the web/email server. A final warning could also be appropriate where the employee has repeatedly failed to heed warnings about not using the email server for private use.

A third category of offence which would be regarded as gross misconduct warranting summary dismissal, could be where there is one single incident of viewing, downloading or distributing sexually offensive material or accessing sites strictly forbidden such as escort or gambling sites: so serious that summary dismissal would be warranted for a first offence.

If employers give examples of what are regarded as inappropriate activities, employees are less likely to be able to convince an Employment Tribunal that they were unaware that what they were doing could lead to dismissal. Examples could be the sending of racially or sexually offensive jokes or religious or homophobic jokes on email or from the web, viewing or downloading sexually or racially offensive material, sending sexually or racially abusive or offensive attachments to other members of staff or to clients.

CASES

In 2004, Telco Cable & Wireless dismissed six members of staff for abuse of its email system, for sending what a spokesperson described as 'obscene' emails which it viewed as an act of serious misconduct.

In *Moonsar* v *Fiveways Express Transport Ltd* [2005] IRLR 9, the Employment Appeal Tribunal explored whether a woman could still suffer sexual harassment even where the sexually offensive materials had not be sent to her and she had not complained about them at the time but where she had knowledge of these activities.

In this case Mrs Moonsar, an office worker, learnt that her male colleagues on three occasions downloaded pornographic images on to screens in the room where they were all working. Although the images were not circulated to Mrs Moonsar, she worked in close proximity and was aware of what was happening. However, she did not complain until after her dismissal, and an employment tribunal rejected her sex discrimination claim.

Allowing an appeal, the EAT said that:

> *viewed objectively, this behaviour ... clearly had the potential effect of causing an affront to a female employee working in the close environment and as such would be regarded as degrading or offensive to an employee as a woman. It was, in our view, clearly potentially less favourable treatment and a detriment clearly followed from the nature of the behaviour, and there was evidence before the tribunal that this lady indeed found that behaviour unacceptable. The fact she did not complain at the time does not, in our view, afford a defence where the behaviour was so obvious, as in this case.*

The EAT went on to find, in the absence of evidence that the claimant was a party to or enjoyed what was going on, that she had been treated less favourably on grounds of sex.

Employers ought to take notice of the *Moonsar* decision. It reflects industrial reality, in which working environments which are sometimes infused with sexual overtones or filled with foul language often with the purpose, and usually with the effect, of making women feel uncomfortable or worse still wanting to get out.

Under the statutory regime which came into force in October 2004, (s. 32 of the Employment Act 2002), Mrs Moonsar would not now be able to bring her sex discrimination complaint unless she had first raised the grievance in writing with her former employer and waited 28 days before presenting a tribunal complaint relating to the matter. The Dispute Resolution Regulations 2004 would now bar her claim unless this process was followed (except where it is not reasonably practicable to follow the procedure).

The *Moonsar* case followed the dicta in *Shamoon* v *Chief Constable of the Royal Ulster Constabulary* [2003] IRLR 285. Here the House of Lords held that a 'detriment' is held to be an act which a reasonable employee might feel places them at a disadvantage with regard to the circumstances in which they work. It is not necessary to demonstrate some physical or economic consequence.

Even where an employee is caught red-handed it will still be important that the employer has clearly banned the use of the internet for unlawful purposes, for example, for downloading pornographic material.

Even where such conduct is listed as an example of 'misconduct' rather than 'gross misconduct', it may still be fair to dismiss for a first offence depending upon the circumstances of the particular case. For example, it may be within the band of reasonable responses for an employer to dismiss a senior HR officer who has breached the 'office porn rules' particularly as they are supposed to lead by example.

In *Hillingdon Borough Council* v *Thomas* [2002] EAT/1317/01/MAA the EAT held that downloading and viewing pornography can be properly regarded as an act of gross misconduct and as such summary dismissal for a first offence can fall within the band of reasonable responses.

In this case Hillingdon dismissed a senior (lead) personnel officer who had been caught accessing pornography on the internet at his computer at work. The staff handbook provided that this amounted to 'misconduct'. The employment tribunal held that whilst it may be misconduct, it was not gross misconduct and so the dismissal was unfair.

The EAT held this finding was perverse, and substituted a finding that it was within the 'band of reasonable responses' for Hillingdon to dismiss a member of staff for gross misconduct for accessing pornography.

This case is very helpful for all employers who dismiss for similar offences, although it must still be borne in mind that the employee must have been told that accessing pornography is prohibited.

In May 1999, Rolls Royce sacked five people at its Bristol office for using its corporate network for sending 'grossly offensive' hardcore porn but which was not child pornography.

Earlier in the month, 14 people had been suspended at the defence and aerospace division of Rolls Royce for sending emails that contained 'inappropriate material'. Nine others were allowed to return to work having been spared dismissal but having received written or oral warnings about their conduct. They were told that any further abuse of the company's email system will result in summary dismissal.

The five dismissals were upheld by the tribunal.

In 2004 Hazel Mahon was dismissed (fairly) by the Co-operative Insurance Society (CIS) after she had abused her internet access at work.

She alleged that she had posted a number of innocuous messages on 'Johnny Thunders Cyber Lounge' asking where she might get hold of music videos for her son. She left her CIS email address in the postings to the site. Soon after she alleged that she started to receive pornographic emails at work. She alleged that the offensive messages were not written by her but by an 'internet stalker' posing as her.

However the Manchester Tribunal was satisfied that she had posted the offensive messages to herself, the content of which was liable to bring the CIS into disrepute.

ADMITTING THE OFFENCE BUT 'IT WAS A MISTAKE'

The case of *Parr* v *Derwentside District Council* [1998], involved allegations that an employee had used his employer's equipment to access a pornographic website. The employee admitted downloading pornographic pictures and video images but claimed it was done accidentally. The Newcastle tribunal decided that the dismissal had followed a careful investigation and rejected Parr's claim of unfair dismissal. Mr Parr's claim of accidentally hitting such sites was undermined by the fact that access was for a considerable period and he had revisited the site on more than one occasion. His dismissal was held to be fair.

However, in *Dunn* v *IBM UK Ltd,* also decided in 1998, a summary dismissal was held to be unfair after an employee admitted accessing pornography via the internet and making printouts of downloaded pictures.

In this case the tribunal felt that it was significant that the employee had admitted the offences without appreciating that the consequence would be his dismissal. The tribunal also felt that proper disciplinary procedures had not been followed. The tribunal found that there was no clear breach of its company policy because the company had never made it clear that such conduct or the admission of such conduct would lead to dismissal.

Although the dismissal was held to be unfair, the applicant's compensation was explicitly reduced by 50 per cent to take account of his misbehaviour.

CRIMINAL CONDUCT

Downloading pornography may be illegal under the Obscene Publications Act 1959 or, where child pornography is involved, under the Protection of Children Act 1978.

Under the Obscene Publications Act it is an offence to publish, whether for gain or not, any article whose effect is to 'deprave and corrupt' those likely to read, see or hear the matter contained or embodied in it. In theory, what is illegal in print or in video is illegal on the internet, and although the Sexual Offences Act 2003 has introduced more specific regulations on, for instance, 'grooming' offences, it is generally accepted that the Obscene Publications Act is far too vague and, in any case, is very rarely enforced. Commentators are generally pessimistic about the potential of statute to have any effect on what can be accessed on the internet.

The Sexual Offences Act 2003 introduced new offences including responding to new challenges posed by twenty-first century technology and by strengthening measures to combat the sexual exploitation and trafficking of children.

In particular the 2003 Act includes sexual offences involving the internet, and 'grooming'. Sexual approaches to children online are increasing. To combat this there is a new offence of meeting a child following sexual grooming, which makes it a crime to befriend a child on the internet or by other means and to meet or intend to meet the child with the intention of abusing them. The maximum sentence is ten years' imprisonment. A new civil preventative order, the Risk of Sexual Harm Order, may be imposed which will prohibit adults from engaging in inappropriate behaviour such as sexual conversations with children online.

The Protection of Children Act 1978 made it an offence to produce, circulate or possess with a view to distribution any indecent photograph of a child under 16. These offences carry a maximum sentence of three years' imprisonment, an unlimited fine or both. The simple possession of an indecent photograph of a child is also an offence and carries a maximum sentence of six months' imprisonment.

Furthermore the Computer Misuse Act 1990 makes hacking into a computer a criminal offence. The Act created three new offences:

- Unauthorised access to computer material;
- Unauthorised access with intent to commit or facilitate commission of further offences;
- Unauthorised modification of computer material.

VICARIOUS LIABILITY FOR CRIMINAL ACTS OF EMPLOYEES

Recently employers have been given an 'alarm call' when dealing with sexual harassment and in particular male employees who seek to harass female members of staff by, for example, stalking them at work and to and from work. As we have seen vicarious liability is a principle that makes an employer liable for the negligent acts or omissions of its employees. But rarely has an employer been found vicariously liable for the criminal acts of his employees.

In *Majrowski* v *Guys and St Thomas' NHS Hospital Trust* [2005] IRLR 350 the Court of Appeal held that employers could be held vicariously liable for the acts of harassment that lead to a prosecution under the Protection from Harassment Act 1997.

The Protection from Harassment Act 1997 provides that 'a person must not pursue a course of conduct – (a) which amounts to harassment of another; and (b) which he knows or ought to know amounts to harassment of the other'.

There is no definition of harassment as such, but the Act stipulates that 'references to harassing a person include alarming the person or causing the person distress', that a 'course of conduct' must involve 'conduct on at least two occasions', and that 'conduct' includes 'speech'. It provides a civil remedy for the harassment, as well as a criminal one, including 'damages for any anxiety caused by the harassment'.

In *Majrowski's* case, Mr Majrowski, a hospital employee, alleged that he was bullied, intimidated and harassed by his departmental manager. On the key issue of principle, the Court of Appeal ruled that employers can be held vicariously liable under the Protection from Harassment Act for their employees' acts of harassment of third parties.

Giving the lead decision, Lord Justice Auld held that:

> *It may be that the principal mischief at which the 1997 Act was directed was the practice of stalking, not something normally done by a person in circumstances that could involve an employer in vicarious liability. Nevertheless, it is plain that the prohibition in s.1 of "a course of conduct ... which amounts to harassment of another" is capable of wider application than to stalkers.*

The Court of Appeal went on to hold, by a majority, that there was nothing in the wording or policy of the Act that prevented an employer being vicariously liable for harassment by its employees, as long as there was a sufficiently close connection with employment.

Lord Justice Auld added that the reasoning in this case would apply:

> *Not only where one employee, in the course of his employment, harasses another employee, but also where an employee, in the course of his employment, harasses an outsider, say a customer of his employer or*

some other third party with whom his work brings him or her into regular contact.

This decision therefore provides an alternative potential remedy against the employer for employees who claim to have been bullied at the workplace, and a remedy that does not require the employee to resign and claim constructive dismissal, or to establish that the bullying was linked to some form of unlawful discrimination. It also provides a potential remedy for those subjected to third party harassment, albeit against the employer of the harasser rather than their own employer.

INTERNET AND EMAIL STALKING

In a survey by Chubb Insurance (7 May 2004) it was reported that stalkers are now using email and the internet to prey on their victims and that one in eight adults in the UK is a victim of stalking. Up until recently this used to be by way of unwanted telephone calls, letters and physical surveillance. With the advent of e-technology, stalkers, according to this report, are taking advantage of email to harass their victims.

In April 2004, Robert James Murphy, from South Carolina was charged with 28 offences of using his computer to harass a female victim. The State laws outlaw internet stalking.

CATCHING THE SEX PESTS IN THE OFFICE

There are now sophisticated software programmes which can identify key words and which can decode slang and codes both in telephone calls and in emails in order for the employer to be able to identify any hint of bullying, discrimination, inappropriate language, swearing or simple time-wasting.

These 'email management solutions' are becoming more popular with employers as a means of prevention rather than cure. One such programme, published by Aungate, intercepts emails and telephone calls which contain suspect words. Another programme, Mimesweeper, detects attachments with nude or semi-nude images.

In Switzerland, companies deal with stricter privacy laws by using software which bounces back potentially offensive emails from workers, and sends a request for them to modify the content before it can be sent again.

BEING CAUGHT BY EMAIL

Emails are durable and admissible evidence in court and have in the past been a major source of evidence that has caught out perpetrators.

The Labour Government was seriously embarrassed over emails disclosed in the Hutton Enquiry into the death of David Kelly. Emails from Tony Blair's office provided significant evidence for the enquiry. These included emails between officials at crucial moments during the Iraq crisis. They disclosed significant insights into the role of the Prime Minister's advisers in compiling the Iraq dossier. This will provide a useful precedent for future Government enquiries where emails will be expected to be disclosed.

At the time of writing, Conrad Black's emails are being used in a claim by one of his former companies for repayment of more than $200 million. The lawsuit accuses him of taking money 'through various improper means' from Hollinger International which controlled his newspaper interests. One of his emails quoted Lord Black as saying that Hollinger 'served no other purpose as a listed company other than relatively cheap use of other people's capital'.

Previously in the USA, Eliot Spitzer, a New York lawyer, had made interesting use of emails in cases against Wall Street abuses. The most infamous email was that written by Henry Blodget of Merrill Lynch describing as 'a piece of shit' a company that Merrill Lynch had publicly recommended.

In April 2004 it was reported that Sir Philip Watts and Walter van de Vijver (both reported in the *Financial Times* as being forced out of top executive positions in Royal Dutch Shell) had engaged in an email dialogue over two years which a non-executive director described as 'ill-considered hyperbolic email chatter'. This emerged following Shell's announcement that a large slice of its reserves was not compliant with Security and Exchange Commission (SEC) rules in February 2002, almost two years before the Company announced its over-statement.

INTERNET USE – DISCRIMINATION, HARASSMENT AND DISMISSAL

Remarks sent by email and lewd images and attachments are all capable of amounting to harassment and of forming the foundation for complaints of discrimination under the Sex or Disability Discrimination Acts, Race Relations Act or the Fair Employment legislation in Northern Ireland. The intention of the parties is irrelevant if the behaviour in question subjects the individual to a detriment and it can be said that the individual has been treated less favourably on account of his or her sex, race and so on.

The employer has a legal duty to protect employees from harassment and may be vicariously liable for such discrimination. In defending claims, it is for the employer to show that it took all reasonably practicable steps to prevent its employees from committing discriminatory acts. This means that any failure to supervise the use of email and deal with problems once they have come to the attention of management increases the risk of liability.

If pornography or other inappropriate material is attached to an email and sent directly to another employee, this may form the basis for a discrimination complaint for which the employer could be vicariously liable. But pornography does not have to be used in such a directly offensive way to give rise to liability.

As the Morse case showed (*Morse* v *Future Reality Ltd* Case No: 54571/95 London North Employment Tribunal, see Chapter 4), employers risk discrimination complaints if they permit employees to create a hostile working environment by downloading and circulating explicit material.

The question may also arise as to whether the employer is entitled to dismiss an employee who uses the internet for wholly unauthorised purposes. Unless an employer's disciplinary or computer-use policy expressly states that the downloading and/or circulation of pornography constitutes gross misconduct, it is unlikely that the mere use of the internet at work for these purposes will be grounds for summary dismissal. However, if the pornographic material is of such an extreme kind as to be regarded as 'obscene' or involves paedophiliac images, then the employee may be committing a criminal offence by downloading or disseminating the material under the Obscene Publications Act 1959 or the Protection of Children Act 1978 (as amended).

As with any other criminal offence committed during working hours involving use of the employer's facilities, the employer may choose to treat the matter as gross misconduct.

CHAPTER 6

Covert Surveillance and Data Protection

INTRODUCTION

According to Bully online (www.bullyonline.org), there have been between 200 000 and 250 000 sales of TV cameras in the UK suitable for covert surveillance.

Covert surveillance and monitoring can take a variety of different forms from monitoring electronic communications, video and audio monitoring, covert monitoring, in-vehicle monitoring and monitoring through information from third parties.

An increasing number of employers seek to monitor the activity of their staff by the use of covert CCTV surveillance, using private investigators or security firms, using software that records the number of keystrokes and then flags up anyone whose typing is not achieving the 'required level'. Employers also log and report internet access, intercept email and duplicate what is on employees' computer monitors on a screen elsewhere.

There are many sensible reasons for employers using CCTV both overtly and covertly – for example, to monitor the premises for intruders, to monitor car parks to ensure the safety of staff, to monitor access and egress to safeguard the security of goods and to monitor the movement of people inside the office as a means of ensuring that their goods and valuables are safe.

However, there are a number of apparently conflicting legal issues in monitoring employees at work. Firstly, any such monitoring must comply with the strict rules under the Data Protection Act 1998. Secondly, Article 8(1) of the Human Rights Act 1998 guarantees individuals the right to respect for their privacy, family life and correspondence. Thirdly, the Telecommunications (Lawful Business Practice) (Interception of Communications) Regulations 2000 requires certain conditions to be met before lawful surveillance can take place.

USE OF CCTV

Under the Data Protection Act 1998 moving images are included in the definition of data. Under Part 3 of the Information Commissioner's code of practice there is comprehensive guidance on monitoring employees at work.

For small users of CCTV, the following checklist has been published by the Information Commissioner.

It is designed to help operators of small CCTV systems comply with the legal requirements of the Data Protection Act 1998 and it details the main issues that need to be addressed when operating a CCTV system. It should help to ensure that the CCTV system remains compliant with the requirements of the Act.

It is important that the Data Protection Act is complied with because failure to do so may result in action being taken under this Act. Failure to comply with data protection requirements will also affect the police's ability to use the CCTV images to investigate a crime and may hamper the prosecution of offenders.

If any employer uses a CCTV system in connection with their business they should work through the checklist and address all the points listed. This will help to ensure that the CCTV system remains within the law and that images can be used by the police to investigate crime.

CHECKLIST FOR USE OF CCTV PRODUCED BY THE INFORMATION COMMISSIONER

A checklist for use of CCTV is shown below.

Operation of the CCTV System

This CCTV equipment and the images recorded by it are controlled by .... who is responsible for how the system is used and for notifying the Information Commissioner about the CCTV system and its purpose (this is a legal requirement of the Data Protection Act 1998).

The above controller has considered the need for using a CCTV system and has decided it is required for the prevention and detection of crime and for protecting the safety of customers. It will not be used for other purposes.

	Checked (Date)	By	Date of next review
The controller is aware that notification to the Information Commissioner is necessary and must be renewed annually.			
Notification has been submitted to the Information Commissioner and the next renewal date recorded.			
Cameras have been sited so that their images are clear enough to allow the police to use them to investigate a crime.			
Cameras have been positioned to avoid capturing the images of persons not visiting the premises.			
There are signs showing that a CCTV system is in operation visible to people visiting the premises and the controller's contact details are displayed on the sign where it is not obvious who is responsible for the system.			
The recorded images from this CCTV system are securely stored, where only a limited number of authorised persons may have access to them			
The recorded images will only be retained long enough for any incident to come to light (for example, for a theft to be noticed).			
Recordings will only be made available to law enforcement agencies involved in the prevention and detection of crime, and no other third parties.			
The operating equipment is regularly checked to ensure that it is working properly (for example, the recording media used is of an appropriate standard and that features on the equipment such as the date and time stamp are correctly set).			
The controller knows how to respond to requests from individuals for access to images relating to that individual. If unsure the controller knows to seek advice from the Information Commissioner as soon as such a request is made.			

Please keep this checklist in a safe place until the date of the next review.

The Data Protection Act 1998 places duties and responsibilities on those who process personal data (whether in paper or electronic form) to safeguard its use and its security and not to keep any personal data for longer than is necessary. This book cannot go into detail into the intricacies of the Data Protection Act 1998.

However in a decision in the Court of Appeal – *Durant* v *Financial Services Authority* [2003] EWCA Civ 1746 – the definition of personal data and what personal data comes within the scope of the Act was revised and clarified.

Only data that is in a real sense biographical can fall under the definition of 'personal data'. So any video images which contain numerous people and which does not concentrate on one person and their activities will not, according to the *Durant* decision, fall under the Act.

RIPA

There is a code of practice under s.71 of RIPA concerning covert surveillance by public authorities.This covers the extent of the powers to use covert surveillance, rules on authorisation and special rules in cases where, for example, legal privilege can be claimed, authorisation procedures and procedures for tapping telephones.

MONITORING UNDER THE DATA PROTECTION ACT 1998

Guidance from the Information Commissioner in Part 3 of the Code of Practice recommends various approaches to monitoring.

Impact assessments lie at the heart of the recommendations in this part of the code of practice. The code recommends that before monitoring is carried out, employers should identify clearly the purpose(s) behind the monitoring and the specific benefits it is likely to bring. An impact assessment will allow an employer to determine whether the likely benefits justify any adverse impact.

Employers are recommended to:

- identify the monitoring that currently takes place in their organization;
- identify any monitoring that they plan to implement;
- consider conducting an impact assessment on either current or planned monitoring;

- If monitoring is to be used to enforce the organization's rules and standards make sure that the rules and standards are clearly set out in a policy which also refers to the nature and extent of any associated monitoring. Ensure workers are aware of the policy.

Employers who ensure that all their workers are fully aware and are kept updated on whether overt and covert monitoring is taking place are more likely to satisfy the requirements of the Data Protection Act 1998 and the code of practice.

CORE PRINCIPLES

- It will usually be intrusive to monitor workers.
- Workers have legitimate expectations that they can keep their personal lives private and that they are also entitled to a degree of privacy in the work environment.
- If employers wish to monitor their workers, they should be clear about the purpose and satisfied that the particular monitoring arrangement is justified by real benefits that will be delivered.
- Workers should be aware of the nature, extent and reasons for any monitoring, unless (exceptionally) covert monitoring is justified.
- In any event, workers' awareness will influence their expectations.

WHO CAN AUTHORISE MONITORING?

It is essential that someone at a senior level is responsible for deciding whether and where and by what means covert or overt surveillance by CCTV should be carried out.

Clearly the person(s) who are authorised to carry out the monitoring must be briefed on the legal requirements and that managers understand the consequences of not complying with the procedure and policy on who may authorise covert surveillance.

IMPACT ASSESSMENTS

The Information Commissioner recommends that before monitoring is carried out, employers should identify clearly the purpose(s) behind the monitoring and the specific benefits it is likely to bring. An impact assessment will allow an employer to determine whether the likely benefits justify any adverse impact.

COVERT SURVEILLANCE

Where covert surveillance needs to be carried for the prevention or detection of crime, employers will not be required to warn staff in advance. However a general policy statement should include the fact that where the employer suspects or has grounds to believe that a crime is being committed, hidden surveillance cameras may be placed on company premises but they will not be placed in any area where the staff have a reasonable expectation of privacy, for example, in the toilets.

The Code of Practice emphasizes that any such rules and standards should be set out in policies that are clearly communicated to workers and that staff are told what monitoring is taking place and why, and keep them aware of this, unless covert monitoring is justified.

This can be done by way of the intranet with regular updates if the policy changes.

Employers are recommended to keep to a minimum those who have access to personal information obtained through monitoring; subject them to confidentiality and security requirements and ensure that they are properly trained where the nature of the information requires this. Most probably security personnel will be in charge of such covert surveillance so it is essential that they are fully trained and aware of their obligations under the Data Protection Act 1998.

Any personal data gained under covert surveillance should only be used for the purposes for which it was collected unless it is in the individual's interests or it reveals activity that no employer could reasonably be expected to ignore.

In one case a covert camera for the purposes of trying to identify a thief who had been stealing from staff revealed that two security staff themselves were opening and reading confidential mail including details of the pay and bonuses of the directors! Both men were dismissed summarily for gross misconduct and a third man was dismissed for standing by and watching!

In another case a hidden camera on the directors' floor designed to catch a thief who was stealing from the offices, revealed a secret assignation between a manager in IT and a director's secretary. It would have breached the Code of Practice if that video footage had been shown to either of the individual's spouses!

In this regard only senior management should be able to authorise the use of personal information obtained through monitoring for new or different purposes.

Staff should have a means of challenging the video footage and bringing a grievance through the grievance procedure if they are unhappy with the quality or content or storage or access to the material. All visitors and contractors should be made aware by way of visible notices if any video monitoring is being carried out and where it is being carried out.

The Data Protection Code of Practice, part 3, defines 'covert monitoring' as monitoring carried out in a manner calculated to ensure those subject to it are unaware that it is taking place. It is recommended that senior management should normally authorize any covert monitoring. They should satisfy themselves that there are grounds for suspecting criminal activity or equivalent malpractice and that notifying individuals about the monitoring would prejudice its prevention or detection. Covert monitoring should be strictly targeted at obtaining evidence within a set timeframe and that the covert monitoring does not continue after the investigation is complete.

In one organization, where collecting money from members of the public in open buckets was the practice (that soon changed), management suspected that those charged with counting and collecting the money were acting dishonestly. Hidden security cameras were therefore placed in the room where the money was counted and stored until the perpetrator was caught. The cameras were then taken out.

EVIDENCE OBTAINED ILLEGALLY

Where evidence has been obtained illegally by means of a covert camera, the courts and tribunals are required to determine whether evidence gained by such means is admissible as evidence.

Employees will argue that Article 8 of the Human Rights Act 1998 has been breached along with their rights under the Data Protection Act 1998. There is an interesting tension between these various statutory rights and protections. Employers will argue that to exclude such evidence is a breach of their Article 6 right – the right to a fair trial.

In *XXX v YYY and ZZZ* [2004] IRLR 471 the case concerned a claim by a nanny that she had been sexually harassed by the father of the child she cared for. She sought to adduce in evidence a video she had covertly made in the kitchen of the family home allegedly showing her being subjected to sexual advances. The video was shot in the kitchen of the family home. The child was in much of the footage, and an issue arose as to whether his human rights would be infringed if the video was played in public.

The Employment Tribunal held that the video was not admissible as evidence because it had no probative value in the sex discrimination case in that it was consistent with the father's case that there was a consensual sexual relationship.

The EAT overruled this on grounds that it was not clear when the sexual relationship ceased so that the conduct depicted in the video might have occurred after that time. The EAT also held that if the video was played in public session, it would infringe the child's right to protection of his private and family life, in that its contents could be described in newspapers and images circulated.

Rule 10(3) of the Rules of Procedure 2001 were used allowing a tribunal to sit in private to hear evidence from any person which is likely to consist of 'information which he could not disclose without contravening a prohibition imposed by or by virtue of any enactment'.

The Employment Appeal Tribunal ruled that hearing the case in public would breach the Human Rights Convention, Article 6, which expressly allows for a case to be heard in private where this is in 'the interests of juveniles or the protection of the private life of the parties'.

The Court of Appeal restored the decision of the Employment Tribunal that the video had no probative value. Lord Justice Buxton emphasized that *'the first and most important rule of the law of evidence ... is that evidence is only admissible if it is relevant to an issue between the parties.'*

In this case, the dispute was as to whether the relationship between the claimant and the father was consensual or not consensual. Since it was not suggested that the relationship was originally unwelcomed and then became consensual, or vice versa, it would not affect the issues between the parties if the conduct shown took place after the date on which the consensual relationship was said to have terminated.

USING PRIVATE DETECTIVES

There is nothing unlawful *per se* about using private detectives to assist in the detection or prevention of crime. They are most commonly used in cases where either the employee has gone on sick leave with or without a claim for personal injuries and there are suspicions about the genuineness of the injury or illness. In other cases private detectives may be used to detect criminal activities such as theft of company goods. Forensic accountants are used in cases where white collar fraud is suspected.

For example, in one firm the Marketing Director had set up dummy accounts and was authorizing cheques for non-existent work made payable to false names and addresses. Forensic accountants caught him out.

The Information Commissioner's guidance on the use of private detectives is clear.

If a private investigator is employed to collect information on workers covertly then there should be a contract in place that requires the private investigator to only collect information in a way that satisfies the employer's obligations under the Act. For example, clear written instructions should be given that there should be no intrusion into the privacy of the individual's home, no interference with correspondence and no illegal telephone tapping of the individual's private/home telephones.

The employer should also satisfy himself about the integrity and professionalism of the private detectives being instructed and should ensure that they are bound by strict rules of confidentiality including obtaining, using and storing information in accordance with the employer's instructions.

Information obtained through covert monitoring should be used only for the prevention or detection of criminal activity or equivalent malpractice. Other information collected in the course of monitoring should be deleted or disregarded unless it reveals information that no employer could reasonably be expected to ignore.

IN-VEHICLE MONITORING

Devices can record or transmit information such as the location of a vehicle, the distance it has covered and information about the user's driving habits.

Monitoring of vehicle movements, where the vehicle is allocated to a specific driver, and information about the performance of the vehicle can therefore be linked to a specific individual, will fall within the scope of the Data Protection Act.

If in-vehicle monitoring is or will be used, consider – preferably using an impact assessment – whether the benefits justify the adverse impact.

The Information Commissioner warns that:

- Where private use of a vehicle is allowed, monitoring its movements when used privately, without the freely given consent of the user, will rarely be justified.

- If the vehicle is for both private and business use, it ought to be possible to provide a 'privacy button' or similar arrangement to enable the monitoring to be disabled.
- Where an employer is under a legal obligation to monitor the use of vehicles, even if used privately, for example, by fitting a tachograph to a lorry, then the legal obligation will take precedence.
- Drivers should be aware of exactly what monitoring devices have been placed in their vehicles.

CHAPTER 7

Data Protection and Freedom of Information

THE DATA PROTECTION ACT 1998 AND FREEDOM OF INFORMATION ACT 2000

The Data Protection Act 1998 places duties and responsibilities on those who process personal data (whether in paper or electronic form) to safeguard its use and its security and not to keep any personal data for longer than is necessary.

This book cannot go into detail into the intricacies of the Data Protection Act 1998 or the Freedom of Information Act 2000 but here is a brief summary.

> *..... whilst I accept that time was taken up with the claimants' claim under the Data Protection Act [1998] which was successful only as to nominal damages, I must recognise, too, that the Act is of notorious obscurity.*
>
> Lindsay J. in *Douglas* v *Hello! Ltd* (No.7) (2004).

BASIC FACTS

- The Data Protection Act was passed in 1998 and came fully into force in 2001.
- It was amended by the Freedom of Information Act (FOIA) 2000 to cover additional issues in relation to public authorities, including colleges and universities.
- The Data Protection Act 1998 covers all personal data processed by a data controller including computerised data, structured manual files and unstructured data, except where specifically exempted.

SUMMARY

The Data Protection Act 1998 gives individuals certain rights regarding information held about them. It places obligations on those who process information (data controllers) while giving rights to those who are the subject of that data (data subjects).

Personal information covers both facts and opinions about the individual. Anyone processing personal information must notify the Information Commissioner's Office (TICO) (http://www.informationcommissioner.gov.uk/) that they are doing so, unless their processing is exempt. Notification costs £35 per year.

THE EIGHT PRINCIPLES – SCHEDULE 1 OF DATA PROTECTION ACT 1998

Anyone processing personal information must comply with eight general principles. These are that data must be:

- fairly and lawfully processed;
- processed for limited purposes;
- adequate, relevant and not excessive;
- accurate and up to date;
- not kept longer than necessary;
- processed in accordance with the individual's rights;
- secure;
- not transferred to countries outside European Economic area unless that country has adequate protection for the individual.

ENFORCEMENT

The Information Commissioner oversees both the Freedom of Information Act 2000 (FOIA) and the Data Protection Act 1998. Both Acts affect information policy and practice.

They overlap where personal information is considered for disclosure. Joint responsibility allows the Information Commissioner to provide a single point of contact for public authorities and the public.

The FOIA 2000 extends the rights of the individual to access their data which had already existed under the Data Protection Act 1998. The definition of 'data' is widened, as far as public authorities are concerned, to include all other 'recorded information held by a public authority'. However, there are limits to the data subject rights that apply to this additional category of data (see below).

A request by an individual for information about him or herself is exempt under the FOIA 2000 and should be handled as a 'subject access request' under the Data Protection Act 1998. In certain circumstances, such a request may involve the release of associated information in which case the provisions of sections 7(4) and (5) of the Data Protection Act 1998 should be used to determine whether it is appropriate to release the third party information.

Where an applicant specifically requests information about a third party, or where responding to a request for information would involve the disclosure of personal information about a third party (which is not also personal information about the applicant), the request falls within the remit of the FOIA 2000. However, the authority must apply the data protection principles when considering the disclosure of information relating to living individuals. An authority must not release third party information if to do so would mean breaching one of the principles.

Where the disclosure would not breach the principles, the authority may release the information. However, if the third party has served notice under s.10 of the Data Protection Act 1998 that disclosure would cause them unwarranted substantial damage or distress, or the third party would not have a right to know about the information relating to them or a right of access to it under the Data Protection Act 1998, the institution is required to consider whether release of the information would be in the public interest.

The Data Protection Act 1998 defines 'personal data' as 'any information that relates to an identified or identifiable person (the data subject), or which in combination with other information in the possession of, or that is likely to come into the possession of, the data controller would permit their identification'.

THE DURANT CASE

This definition of 'personal data' was considered by the UK Court of Appeal in the case of *Durant* v *Financial Services Authority* [2003] EWCA Civ 1746.

In *Durant* the Court of Appeal did not consider the issue of the 'identifiability' of an individual, but concentrated on the meaning of 'relate to'. The Court decided that data will relate to an individual if it: 'is information that affects [a person's] privacy, whether in his personal or family life, business or professional capacity'.

The Court identified two issues that may aid in determining whether information 'is information that affects [an individual's] privacy' and, thus, 'relates to' an individual:

> *... whether the information is biographical in a significant sense that is, going beyond the recording of [the individual's] involvement in a matter or an event which has no personal connotations.*
>
> *... The information should have the [individual] as its focus rather than some other person with whom he may have been involved or some transaction or event in which he may have figured or have had an interest .*

If an individual's name appears in information, the use of the name implicates 'personal data' only where its inclusion affects the named individual's privacy. Thus, the fact that an individual's name appears on a document, does not mean the information contained in that document will necessarily be personal data about the named individual. It is more likely that an individual's name will be 'personal data' where the name appears together with other information about the named individual such as address, telephone number or information regarding his hobbies.

The Information Commissioner suggests that the following examples of information will not normally be personal data:

- mere reference to a person's name where it is not associated with any other personal information;
- incidental mention in the minutes of a business meeting of an individual's attendance at that meeting in an official capacity;
- where an individual's name appears on a document or email indicating only that it has been sent or copied to that particular individual – and there is no other information about the individual within it.

The Court of Appeal also considered the definition of 'relevant filing system' and held that it was to be more narrowly construed than had been previously advised by the Information Commissioner.

A 'relevant filing system' is a 'system':

- in which files are structured or referenced so as to clearly indicate at the outset of the search whether specific information capable of amounting to personal data of an individual making a subject access request is held within the system and, if so, in which file or files it is held; and

- which has, as part of its own structure or referencing mechanism, a sufficiently sophisticated and detailed means of readily indicating whether and where in an individual file or files specific criteria or information about the applicant can be readily located.

The Information Commissioner has now suggested using what it calls the 'temp test' to assess manual filing systems. In other words, if an institution employed a reasonably competent temporary administrative assistant, would they be able to extract specific information about an individual without any particular knowledge of the work that the institution does or the documents that it holds, after only a short induction, explanation and/or operating manual on the particular filing system? If a temp could locate the information easily, the information will be held in a relevant filing system. The Information Commissioner's guidance notes that very few manual files are currently likely to be caught by the Data Protection Act 1998 under this definition.

THE FOIA 2000 AMENDMENT

The FOIA 2000 amends the Data Protection Act 1998 as to the scope of personal data which must be released under a data subject access request.

EXEMPTIONS TO DATA SUBJECT ACCESS REQUESTS

The exemptions to data subject access requests are:

- request is not in writing;
- required fee is not received;
- data subject is not able to verify identity upon request;
- disclosure would require disclosure of third party's personal data, and third party has not consented where it would be reasonable to require consent;
- disclosure would require disclosure of third party as source of personal data, and third party has not consented where it would be reasonable to require consent;
- exemptions in secondary legislation (for example, regarding certain health records, school educational records, social work records).

OBLIGATIONS ON THOSE WHO CONTROL THE PROCESSING OF DATA

PROCESSING

Schedule 2 of the Data Protection Act 1998 lists specific conditions for all processing of personal data and Schedule 3 of the Data Protection Act 1998 lists specific conditions for the processing of 'sensitive' personal data.

THE SIX CONDITIONS

For 'ordinary' personal data, at least one of the following conditions must be met for personal information to be considered fairly processed. The conditions are:

- the individual has consented to the processing;
- processing is necessary for the performance of a contract with the individual;
- processing is required under a legal obligation (other than a contractual one);
- processing is necessary to protect the vital interests of the individual;
- processing is necessary to carry out public functions, for example, administration of justice;
- processing is necessary in order to pursue the legitimate interests of the data controller or third parties and is not unfair to the individual.

For 'sensitive' personal data, one of the ordinary processing conditions and one of the conditions for processing sensitive data must be met before processing can be carried out. The conditions for processing sensitive data are that the data subject has given his or her explicit consent to the processing of the personal data, or that the processing is necessary for a further set of specified reasons, including:

- it is required by law for employment purposes;
- it is needed in order to protect the vital interests of the individual or another person;

- it is needed in connection with the administration of justice or legal proceedings.

The precise meanings of 'consent' and 'explicit consent' are undefined in the 1998 Act, although the Code of Practice, part 4, and the supplemental guidance give more detailed interpretation of 'explicit consent'. Explicit consent must be 'in writing', 'informed' and not given 'under any duress'. If no consent is given and the purpose of particular processing is not otherwise on the list of permissible reasons, use of the personal data will be unlawful.

DATA SUBJECT RIGHTS

The Act gives rights to individuals in respect of personal data held about them by their employers. These include the rights:

- to make subject access requests about the nature of the information and to discover to whom it has been disclosed;
- to prevent processing likely to cause damage or distress;
- to prevent processing for the purposes of direct marketing;
- to be informed about the mechanics of any automated decision-taking process that will significantly affect them;
- not to have significant decisions that affect them made solely by an automated decision-taking process;
- to take action for compensation if they suffer damage by any contravention of the Act by the data controller;
- to take action to rectify, block, erase or destroy inaccurate data;
- to request the Information Commissioner to make an assessment as to whether any provision of the Act has been contravened.

Failure to respect these rights may lead to civil or criminal action against the data controller as an institution and, in circumstances where senior management are considered to have consented to, colluded in, or been negligent over, breaches of the Act, they may be individually prosecuted.

EXEMPTIONS

The Act provides wide exemptions for journalistic, artistic, or literary purposes that would otherwise be in breach of the law. These exemptions apply if the processing is with a view to publication and the data controller reasonably believes both that publication would be in the public interest and that to comply with the relevant data protection provisions would be incompatible with the special purposes.

The 'journalist' exemption was raised as a defence in the cases of *Campbell* v *MGN* [2004] UKHL 22 and *Douglas and Zeta Jones* v *Hello and ors* [2005] EWCA Civ 595. While the Douglases won nominal damages under the Data Protection Act 1998, neither case added much to general understandings about the Act, either in terms of exemptions, or in terms of what constitutes 'significant damage or distress'. It is in any case unlikely that academic research and publishing will normally have recourse to this set of exemptions.

In the *Douglas* case, the Court of Appeal held that:

> (1) The unauthorised photographs of Michael Douglas's wedding reception plainly portrayed aspects of the private life of Michael Douglas and fell within the protection of the law of confidentiality, as extended to cover private or personal information,
>
> (2) The unauthorised photographs invaded the area of privacy which Michael Douglas had chosen to retain and Michael Douglas not '*OK*' (the rival publishers) had the right to protect that area of privacy or confidentiality.'

While there is a wide range of other exemptions, most of those are inapplicable to the activities of most employers on a general basis but may be used in specific cases, for example, if disclosure without consent is required to the police or for legal proceedings.

DISCLOSURE TO THIRD PARTIES

The Data Protection Act 1998 permits the disclosure of an individual's personal data by an institution, even without their consent, where that disclosure is carried out in accordance with the Schedule 2 and 3 conditions for processing and where the data subject has been informed that such disclosure may occur.

The Data Protection Act 1998 itself does not oblige employers to disclose personal data to specific third parties, but s.35(1) states that personal data are exempt from the non-disclosure provisions where the disclosure is required by or under any enactment, by any rule of law or by the order of a court.

Certain third parties may therefore require disclosure of an individual's personal data by an employer. Employers should however, where possible, ensure that their staff or other third parties are properly warned of any known statutory disclosures that they are required to make.

Compliance with the Data Protection Act 1998 requires organisations to consider the implications of many aspects of their operations, both in administration and in teaching. The compliance issues listed below are thus not exhaustive.

In order to safeguard data and in particular 'sensitive data' listed in s.2 of the Act, employers might find it useful to include a confidentiality agreement or clause into the contract of staff such as Human Resources, IT, secretarial staff to senior management and so on.

EXAMPLE OF WORDING OF A CONFIDENTIALITY AGREEMENT FOR HR STAFF

DATE

To: Name/Address/Staff number

RE: DUTY OF CONFIDENTIALITY

During the course of your employment you will have access to, gain knowledge of and/or be entrusted with confidential information concerning, for example, members of staff, clients or potential clients, contractors or matters relating to the Company's business or the business or personal details of one or more of the senior directors/officers of the Company. This information may include matters of a highly sensitive and/or personal nature.

This information is mainly kept in manual personnel files and on computer in electronic form. You will also send and receive emails of a highly confidential nature and with those emails may be attachments in Word or Excel or Powerpoint.

Some of this information is 'sensitive' data under s.2 of the Data Protection Act 1998, for which we have very special duties in particular to keep this sensitive data highly secure and confidential because of the damage and harm that could be done to that individual if misused or disclosed to unauthorised persons. The Information Commissioner has published parts 1 and 2 of a code of practice in 2003 which contain recommended good practice concerning such sensitive data. We expect you to read and follow such recommended good practice.

We as a company have always required our staff to conduct themselves to standards of excellence and for this reason we are asking all staff who have access to any confidential or sensitive data to sign confidentiality agreements in order to ensure that everyone is committed to these standards of excellence. For example, no-one should disclose who has come to the HR department for a meeting or for advice nor of course should the contents of that meeting ever be disclosed other than to authorised members of staff. If in doubt ALWAYS ASK BEFORE DOING ANYTHING AND NEVER GIVE ANY CONFIDENTIAL INFORMATION BY TELEPHONE, FOR EXAMPLE, EMPLOYEES' ADDRESSES OR PERSONAL TELEPHONE NUMBERS. ALWAYS ASK FOR ANY REQUEST TO BE PUT IN WRITING AND REPLY IN WRITING IN ORDER TO ENSURE THE CORRECT IDENTITY OF THE RECIPIENT AND DESTINATION OF THAT INFORMATION.

You should understand that you have access to this information in the course of and because of your employment in our HR department and therefore a trusted member of staff in a very privileged position. Abusing this position would be regarded as a very serious matter.

Informing anyone either within or outside the Company of any matters relating to the Company or its staff and/or their personal details would be regarded as a serious breach of confidentiality and as such could lead to your summary dismissal.

By your signing below, you agree that you will not at any time, whether during or after your employment with the Company, disclose to any unauthorised person within or outside the Company, or make use of such information.

> This duty includes keeping strictly confidential the names and other details relating to individuals, and the making and attending of meetings.
>
> Signed...
> Date ....
> General Counsel
>
> I understand my duty of confidentiality in connection with my work within HR and agree not at any time to disclose to any person not authorised to be informed or otherwise make use of such confidential information as described above.
>
> Signed...
> Date............
> Employee

This agreement could be modified for IT managers and staff who by the nature of their role have access to passwords and highly confidential data.

DISCLOSURE TO THE DATA SUBJECT IN LEGAL PROCEEDINGS

Whilst the Data Protection Act 1998 (s.15(2)) does not contain any general prohibition on a data subject obtaining disclosure under the Civil Procedure Rules (CPR) for specific disclosure – particularly where the claim is for breaches of the data protection principles, the court must exercise its discretion to order specific disclosure. In exercising its discretion the court should bear in mind the concern of the legislation in that provision which was that confidential information relating to a third party should not be disclosed to a data subject.

In *Johnson* v *Medical Defence Union* [2004] EWHC 2509 (Ch) Dr Johnson sought an order for specific disclosure after the MDU refused to renew his membership. Dr Johnson alleged that improper use had been made of his personal data. Dr Johnson made a data subject access request under the Data Protection Act 1998 which the MDU refused.

Dr Johnson challenged the MDU's decision under s.7(9) of the Data Protection Act 1998 complaining of the inadequacy of the MDU's compliance with his request.

The High Court had to decide whether or not to order the MDU to disclose those documents under the CPR for specific disclosure. The MDU resisted the order and argued (successfully) that the balance of s.7 and 15(2) had to be in favour of protecting the confidential data of third parties. In this case the High Court also followed the decision in *Durant* ruling that the manual records did not consist of a structured set of records within a relevant filing system.

DATA MATCHING

Data matching is the computerised comparison of two or more sets of records which relate to the same individual. It is primarily used as a method for combating fraud.

There is increasing use of data matching by both public and private organizations in an attempt to reduce fraudulent activity which has been estimated to run annually into billions of pounds in the UK. The relative cheapness and availability of sophisticated processing means that data matching is likely to increase even more rapidly.

There are a number of examples of data matching being undertaken by government agencies. The Department of Social Security (DSS) has established a Housing Benefit Matching Service aimed at detecting benefit fraud.

The Audit Commission uses data matching across local authorities regarding benefit claims, education awards and activities of local authority employees. The Social Security Administration (Fraud) Bill provides for wider sharing by central and local government and the Post Office for fraud prevention or detection purposes.

There is a difference between the methods of fraud detection used in the past and data matching. Traditional investigation is triggered by some evidence of a wrongdoing by an individual, such as tax evasion or bogus benefit claims. Data matching is not targeted at individuals but at entire categories of people. It is initiated not by the suspicion concerning an individual but because the profile of a particular group is of interest. This leads to three issues of concern.

- *Privacy* – Data matching is likely to involve matching personal records compiled for unrelated purposes. Surely an individual has a right to control personal information and prevent its use without consent for purposes unrelated to those for which it was collected.

- *Due process of the law* – Once a match has been undertaken it will result in a number of hits. All those identified are in jeopardy of being found guilty of wrongdoing. It is unlikely that these individuals are given any notice of their situation, since doing so might affect the investigation, or an opportunity to contest the results of the match at an early stage. For these reasons their right to due process of law is curtailed.
- *Presumption of innocence* – The presumption of innocence is intended to protect people against having to prove that they are free from guilt whenever they are investigated. Data matching can reverse this to a presumption of guilt. This is because the technology of data matching is so plausible and the detection of fraud is much applauded. These powerful influences will weigh heavily in favour of the notion that those identified must be guilty.

One of the advances in data matching techniques is the automatic sharing of information. This is dependent on increasingly complex and expanding communication networks that link more and more organizations together. There is a tendency to view people as objects to be moved about these networks.

In this instance it is unclear how an innocent citizen might be assured that incorrect information is totally corrected or removed across the complex web of organizational relationships. The security of such a network is also of concern as the network will only be as secure as its least secure node. Individual organizations might not be aware of all other organizations linked to the network for if they were they might be wary of sharing information due to insecurity through either technological deficiencies or moral attitudes of some organizations.

In order to detect sophisticated fraud there is a need to use complex data analysis techniques which may well involve methods based on partial match interpretation which in turn increases the risks of incorrect hits. Simple fraud detection lends itself to data matching systems that have little or no human intervention and the pressure to use such systems will grow. There needs to be a clear understanding of who has access to this information and how it will be used. Legislative frameworks, codes of practice and operational procedures must be in place to ensure that data matching is applied in a balanced way sensitive to the needs of organizations and society as a whole and to the rights of individuals.

Many people are probably the subject of some data matching exercise quite frequently. It might be related to a mortgage application or a latest tax return or many other reasons.

In *R* v *(1) c (2) d ex parte A* [2000] QBD 25.10.2000 the police had shared data with a Local Education Authority (LEA) about the homosexual activities of a school teacher 'A'.

'A' had been made a conditional offer of employment as a school teacher. Two police forces were asked to perform a child access vetting enquiry. They were done and non-conviction information was given to the LEA that there had been complaints in two other parts of the country about allegedly inappropriate behaviour (that A had attempted to commit indecent acts) towards pupils. These complaints had been investigated but no charges had ever been brought.

As a result the offer of employment was withdrawn. 'A' challenged the disclosure of such information arguing that it should only take place where there was a pressing need supported by reliable evidence. He contended that there had been illegal disclosure in breach of the Data Protection Act 1998.

His complaints were dismissed by the High Court. They held that there was no breach of the Data Protection Act 1998 because one of the exemptions to the processing of sensitive personal data is where it is disclosed with a view to entering into a contract or that disclosure is necessary for the exercise of functions of a public nature exercised in the public interest.

HOLDING AND PROCESSING DATA

The Data Protection Act 1998 covers all personal data processed by employers including computerised data, structured manual files and unstructured manual data, except where specifically exempted.

It is important to:

- Review and ensure that notification is accurate, and that information provided to data subjects in collection notices is appropriate.
- Audit the accuracy and security of both computer files and manual filing systems, and, where possible, work to reduce duplication of information within an institution to avoid inaccuracies and inconsistencies.
- Ensure that record management systems are suitable to support current institutional data protection and FOI requirements, and that appropriate document lifecycle processes are properly adhered to and audited.

- Ensure that all staff receive data protection and FOI training appropriate to their positions, and that refresher and update training is provided as necessary to guarantee continuing institutional compliance at all levels.
- Ensure that all communications from the Information Commissioner, especially those relating to notification and compliance issues are passed on to, and dealt with expeditiously by, the appropriate institutional officeholder. Failure to respond to communications about non-compliance may lead to both the institution and senior management being prosecuted.

RETENTION OF PERSONNEL RECORDS

The Chartered Institute of Personnel Development (CIPD) has published guidance in the form, of a checklist as to the retention periods for different types of data (revised in December 2004). Principle 5 of Schedule 1 of the 1998 Act requires that 'Personal data processed for any purpose or purposes shall not be kept for longer than is necessary for that purpose or those purposes'.

The checklist is divided into two parts:

- Records for which there are statutory retention periods, with the statutory authorities given.
- Records for which no statutory retention periods exist, but for which recommended retention periods are given. Where the recommended retention period is six years, this is based on the six-year time limit within which legal proceedings must be commenced as laid down under the Limitation Act 1990. Thus, where documents may be relevant to a contractual claim, it is recommended that these be retained for at least the corresponding six-year limitation period.

The Chartered Institute of Personnel and Development (CIPD) provides a checklist of recommended retention periods for various classes of personnel documents, based on current legal requirements and good personnel practice.[1]

COMPUTERISED PERSONNEL RECORDS

There is no legislation to prevent such personnel records being retained in computerised or microfilmed format, but there are some points which should be considered if selecting this method of record keeping.

1 A current version of this factsheet may be accessed at http://www.cipd.co.uk/subjects/hrpract/psnlrecrd/retrecords.htm.

Firstly, computerised records have long been subject to data protection legislation. Employers storing personnel data in this way must comply with strict regulations and be aware of the restrictions on the disclosure of and access to such data. Employees have the right to access their electronically-held records and the employer is under an obligation to ensure that the data is accurate. Before releasing such data to a third party the employer must seek the permission of the individual concerned.

RECENT DATA PROTECTION LEGISLATION

The Data Protection Act 1998 became law on 1 March 2000. This Act incorporates the 1995 European Union Data Protection Directive and will have an impact on record-keeping and access, not only to computerised data, but also for the first time, to manual records. The Act covers both and manual and computerised records, introducing a new category of sensitive data and giving staff greater access to personnel records. Employers should already be reviewing their arrangements for collecting and storing data in line with the proposed provisions.

ACCESS TO PERSONNEL RECORDS

From 24 October 2001, most personnel records, whether held in paper, microform, or computerised format, are subject to data protection legislation. Since that date, all computerised systems have been fully covered by the law, as have manual systems with information held on or after 24 October 1998. Employers storing personnel data must comply with strict regulations and be aware of the restrictions on the disclosure of and access to such data.

Subject to certain exceptions (as detailed in Schedule 7 of the Data Protection Act 1998) employees have the right to access their records and the employer is under an obligation to ensure that the data is accurate. Before releasing such data to a third party the employer must seek the permission of the individual concerned.

In October 2000, the Information Commissioner issued a draft code of practice on employee data for public consultation. Subsequently, the Commissioner has published it as *The Employment Practices Data Protection Code*. It is in four parts:

- Part 1: Recruitment and selection
- Part 2: Employment records
- Part 3: Monitoring at work
- Part 4: Information about workers health.

The various parts of the code, together with additional guidance notes are available on the Information Commissioner's website.

CONCLUSION

Retention of records is a complex area. Companies following good practice would ideally have a document retention policy and monitoring programme that is communicated to all staff. These would encompass the regulations above. This may involve training, not only about the legal issues involved, but also why having organised records benefits the business. Senior management will need to show a commitment to ensure that these procedures are followed.

NEW TECHNOLOGY

Organizations are constantly seeking to improve administrative processes, and the delivery of service. New technologies are constantly being developed and adopted to facilitate those objectives. In recent years, the use of 'smart cards' as an integrated solution to issues such as building security, facilities usage, ID and campus payment systems has been a popular option. All of these processes require careful planning to ensure that the personal data collections and transfers they may generate are handled in conformity with the Data Protection Act 1998.

When planning new systems it is important to:

- Identify the types of data collected, the purposes for which they are processed, and the appropriate Schedule 2 & 3 criteria to legitimise that processing.
- Clarify the roles of those involved in the processing – data subjects, data controllers, data processors – and what their rights and obligations are.
- Ensure that individuals are adequately informed as to why their personal data is being collected, the purpose it will be used for, and the types of party it may be transferred to.
- Ensure that where necessary, consent or explicit consent can be obtained for proposed uses of personal data, and that should individuals withdraw consent for the processing of their personal data, as the Act permits, this can be achieved quickly and effectively.

RESEARCH DATA

The processing of any information relating to an identifiable living individual, including research, constitutes 'personal data processing' and is subject to the Data Protection Act 1998 including the eight data protection principles, (see p.74). However, the Data Protection Act 1998 provides certain exemptions for 'research purposes' including statistical or historical purposes. If the processing is not used to support measures or decisions targeted at particular individuals and it does not cause substantial distress or damage to a data subject, it is exempt from:

- the second principle, meaning that personal data can be processed for purposes other than for which they were originally obtained;
- the fifth principle, meaning that personal data can be held indefinitely;
- the data subject's right of access to his personal data, where the data is processed for research purposes and the results do not identify data subjects.

In addition to the restrictive criteria in Schedule 3 of the Data Protection Act 1998 (explicit consent, medical research by a health professional, equal opportunities monitoring), the Data Protection (Processing of Sensitive Personal Data) Order 2000 expressly permits processing of sensitive personal data for research purposes 'in the substantial public interest' where the sensitive personal data are not used to support measures or decisions targeted at particular individuals without their explicit consent; and no substantial damage or distress is caused, or is likely to be caused, to any person by the keeping of those data.

It is important to remember that:

- While some exemptions are granted for the use of personal data for research purposes, neither the Data Protection Act 1998 nor the Data Protection (Processing of Sensitive Personal Data) Order provides a blanket exemption from all the data protection principles.
- There should be an adequate institutional review process, in advance of use of personal data for research purposes, to ensure that the Data Protection Act 1998 can be adhered to; research should also be periodically monitored/audited for continuing compliance.
- Requirements for appropriate security of data must be respected, including appropriate levels of security for sensitive data and security of data processed by researchers outside the institution.

- Data may not be transferred to researchers in countries outside the EEA unless that country has adequate data protection regulations, or the explicit consent of data subject has been obtained, or there is an appropriate data protection contract with the recipient of the data.
- Research data subjects should still be informed of any new purposes of data processing and the identity of the data controller and any disclosures that may be made.
- Research data subjects must be able meaningfully exercise their right to object to the data processing because it would cause/has caused, them significant damage or distress.

MARKETING

Organizations wishing to use unsolicited electronic marketing communications for purposes such as alumni development and the solicitation of commercial/corporate sponsorship, must be aware of the new UK Privacy and Electronic Communications (EC Directive) Regulations 2003. These provide that:

- Unsolicited marketing calls should not be made to individual subscribers who have opted out either directly or by registering with the central stop-list, the Telephone Preference Service (TPS), or to corporate subscribers (for example companies) who have objected either directly or by registering on the Corporate TPS.
- Unsolicited marketing faxes should not be sent to individuals without their prior consent or to any subscriber who has objected, either directly or by registering on the Fax Preference Service (FPS).
- Unsolicited marketing emails or SMS should not be sent to any individual subscriber who has not consented unless the email address or phone number was collected in the context of a commercial relationship.

SOME KEY DEFINITIONS

Some important definitions relevant to data protection are given below.

DATA SUBJECT

The Data Protection Act 1998 defines a data subject as an individual who is the subject of personal data.

PERSONAL DATA

The Data Protection Act 1998 is only concerned with 'personal data', that is, information relating to a living individual who can be identified from that data, or from that data and other information which is in the possession of, or is likely to come into the possession of, the data controller, including any expression of opinion about the individual and any indication of the intentions of the data controller or any other person in respect of the individual. Data concerning corporate bodies are excluded from the DPA, as are data concerning individuals who have died.

CONSENT

The Data Protection Act 1998 does not contain a definition of consent. If a data subject's consent is to be relied on to provide a Sch.2 criterion (Sch.2, s.1) for lawful processing, then the fact of consent cannot be simply assumed by a data controller (for example where a data controller sends out a form stating that in the absence of a negative response from a data subject their consent will be assumed). Where there is obvious inequality of bargaining power between the data controller and data subject, it may also be difficult to demonstrate the 'freely given' element of consent. Equally, consent may be withdrawn by the data subject at any point, a fact that may prove problematic for data controllers where consents are obtained for data processing purposes without which the data controller cannot provide an essential service. In such circumstances, reliance on another Sch.2 criterion, such as contract, would be more practical.

DATA CONTROLLER

A data controller is 'a person who (either alone or jointly or in common with other persons) determines the purposes for which, and the manner in which, any personal data are, or are to be, processed'. The fact that an individual or institution holds or processes personal data does not make them a data controller, if they do not determine the purpose and manner of that holding or processing.

DATA CONTROLLER IN COMMON

Data controllers who share personal data on data subjects for different purposes are referred to as 'data controllers in common'. Each data controller remains individually responsible for the processing they have carried out on the personal data.

JOINT DATA CONTROLLER

Data controllers who share personal data on data subjects for the same purpose, and who would be jointly liable for any breach under the Data Protection Act 1998, are referred to as 'joint data controllers'.

DATA PROCESSOR

A data processor is any person, other than an employee of the data controller, who processes the data on behalf of the data controller. An employee of the data controller is regarded by the Data Protection Act 1998 as constituting part of the data controller. A data processor has no statutory obligations under the Data Protection Act 1998 as regards processing it carries out on behalf of the data controller. The Data Protection Act 1998 places the burden for ensuring that data processors do not allow breaches of the Act upon the data controllers who use them. Data controllers thus need to ensure that their relationship with a data processor is governed by a formal data processing agreement.

DATA PROCESSING

Data processing is 'obtaining, recording or holding the data or carrying out any operation or set of operations on the data'. This includes collection, recording, organization, storage, adaptation or alteration, retrieval, consultation, use, disclosure by transmission, dissemination or otherwise making available, alignment or combination, blocking, erasure or destruction. It is irrelevant whether these actions are manual or automated. The breadth of the Data Protection Act 1998 definition effectively means that from the moment of its collection, to the moment that it is destroyed or fully anonymised, personal data is being processed and must thus be treated in accordance with the Act.

SENSITIVE PERSONAL DATA

Sensitive personal data are personal data relating to racial or ethnic origin, political opinions, religious beliefs, membership of trade union organisations, physical or mental health, sexual life, offences or alleged offences.

CHAPTER 8

Human Rights and Monitoring Employees

RIGHT TO RESPECT FOR PRIVACY, FAMILY LIFE AND CORRESPONDENCE – ARTICLE 8

Article 8 of the Human Rights Act 1998 provides a general right to respect for privacy where none previously existed. Article 8(1) offers general protection for a person's private and family life, home and correspondence from arbitrary interference by the State or any organ of the State.

This right affects a large number of areas of life ranging from surveillance, monitoring private emails and correspondence to being permitted without discrimination to enjoy all the same rights as heterosexuals with regard to homosexuals, transsexuals and transvestites and so on, as this Article is drafted extremely broadly.

However, the right to respect for these aspects of privacy under Article 8 is qualified. This means that interferences by the State can be permissible, but such interferences must be justified and satisfy certain conditions. Any interference with such a right must be:

- in accordance with law;
- in the interests of the legitimate objectives identified in Article 8(2); and
- necessary in a democratic society.

IN ACCORDANCE WITH LAW

In many cases decided by the European Court of Human Rights (ECHR), interferences with privacy have been in breach of Article 8 because they have not satisfied this first condition. In order for an interference to be in accordance with law, the interference must have a proper legal basis, such as a piece of legislation or rules of a professional body. The law or rule must be understandable, detailed and clear enough to allow a person to regulate his or her behaviour – a secret, unpublished memo in a government department will not suffice, for example. Some well-known scenarios involving interference that could not be justified under Article 8(2) have been the telephone tapping, or bugging, of individuals by the police using procedures and systems not authorised expressly by statute.

THE LEGITIMATE OBJECTIVES

The second condition that the interference must satisfy is that it must pursue an identified legitimate aim. The legitimate objectives set out in Article 8(2) are:

- acting in the interests of national security, public safety or the economic wellbeing of the country;
- acting for the prevention of disorder or crime;
- acting for the protection of health or morals;
- acting for the protection of the rights and freedoms of others.

These objectives are widely drawn and it will often be possible for an interference to be categorized as being in pursuit of one of these legitimate objectives, for example, telephone tapping for the purposes of investigation or prevention of crime. More difficult questions arise where there are competing interests at issue, such as balancing privacy rights against the right of freedom of expression in cases of publication of photographs or materials about a person's private life. In some cases it will be important to distinguish between a lawful interference in someone's private life in the public interest, as opposed to an unlawful one which has occurred merely because it is something in which the public might be interested.

NECESSARY IN A DEMOCRATIC SOCIETY

Even if the infringement of privacy is in accordance with the law, and it is for one of the legitimate objectives, it must still be 'necessary' in order for it to be justified under Article 8. This is the third and most stringent condition that any infringement must satisfy, bringing in a requirement that the act must be 'proportionate'.

The requirement of proportionality is often described as 'not using a sledgehammer to crack a nut'. In essence, this means that the nature and extent of each interference must be judged against the end it is meant to achieve and any interference with rights under Article 8 that goes further than is necessary may well be unlawful. For example, a blanket policy of excluding prisoners during examinations of their legally privileged correspondence was considered a disproportionate interference with their rights to privacy and correspondence under Article 8.

The more severe the infringement of privacy, the more important the legitimate objective in each case will need to be. In most cases, the interference will be judged against whether it meets a pressing social need, and the extent to which an alternative, less intrusive interference would achieve the same result.

SCOPE OF RIGHTS PROTECTED BY ARTICLE 8

The right to respect for private and family life, home and correspondence in Article 8 brings wider protection than might be thought at first glance.

Respect for private life includes a right to develop one's own personality, as well as to create relationships with others. For example, Article 8 has been essential in providing basic protection for the rights of homosexuals and transsexuals (see *Lustig Prean* v *United Kingdom* [2000] 29 EHRR 548 European Court of Human Rights – four army officers who were dismissed when the Army learnt of their homosexuality successfully challenged their dismissals as being a breach of Article 8 and 10 – freedom of expression).

Other issues to consider include confidentiality, abortion issues and transsexuals. *R* v *North West Lancashire Health Authority ex parte A* and others where the authority's policy on gender reassignment surgery was called into question. The applicants sought to rely on Article 8 but they were all successful on domestic principles, largely because the authority had a blanket policy which did not treat each case on its merits.

Covert surveillance, for example in relation to use of CCTV in criminal investigations in NHS Trusts or clinical situations would also fall under this Article and the Government's Regulation of Investigatory Powers Act 2000 provides the statutory framework for such interference.

THE DUTY OF PUBLIC AUTHORITIES

The requirement on public authorities to act compatibly with Article 8 of the Convention is contained in section 6 of the Human Rights Act 1998. Section 6 provides that central government, local government and other public bodies such as the police and the courts must all act compatibly with an individual's rights.

There is still no general right to protection from invasion of privacy by other individuals in society. However, the right to respect for privacy under the Data Protection Act 1998 and Article 8, was explored in the case of *Naomi Campbell* v *Mirror Group Newspapers Ltd* in the House of Lords, which upheld her claim that she had a right to respect for privacy. In this case the *Mirror* had photographed her coming out of a Narcotics Anonymous (NA) clinic. The accompanying story included the fact that she had claimed publicly that she did not take drugs.

The House of Lords restored her modest award of damages under the Data Protection Act 1998 by the High Court Judge, Mr Justice Morland. He had held that the Mirror Group must have known that the information about Miss Campbell's attendance at NA was confidential and that there was no overriding public interest in publication.

Miss Campbell's case was that information about the details of the treatment she was receiving for addiction at NA and an accompanying photograph were entitled to protection by reason of their private nature because in relation to that information her right to privacy under the European Convention on Human Rights 1950 Article 8 outweighed the competing interest of the Mirror's freedom of expression under Article 10.

The House of Lords held that the judge was right that the information in issue was all private and confidential. The Mirror Group ought to have known that there was a reasonable expectation that the information in question would be kept confidential (*A* v *B & anor* (2002) EWCA Civ 337, (2002) EMLR 371 approved).

The Court of Appeal was wrong to hold that the peripheral information was within the margin of appreciation which should be left to journalists and that Mirror Group's freedom of expression served to justify the publication of all the information. The publication of the fact that Miss Campbell had taken drugs and was seeking treatment was necessary to set the record straight given her previous statements, but the additional information including the photograph was an unjustified intrusion into her private life.

Balancing the competing interests, her right to privacy under Article 8 outweighed the Mirror's freedom of expression under Article 10.

HALFORD'S CASE IN EUROPEAN COURT OF HUMAN RIGHTS (ECHR)

Alison Halford tested her right to respect for privacy in her successful claim to the ECHR – *Halford* v *United Kingdom* [1997] IRLR 471 after her telephone had been tapped by her employers. In this case, Alison Halford was a very senior police officer in the Merseyside Police Authority. She sued her employers for sex discrimination following several unsuccessful attempts to be promoted. She had a private telephone in her office upon which she used to speak to her lawyers. Unbeknownst to her, her employers had tapped this telephone and therefore learnt of legally privileged information in advance of the trial.

Ms Halford successfully sued Merseyside Police Authority.

The European Court of Human Rights held:

The interception by her employers of calls made on the applicant's office telephones was a violation of Article 8 of the European Convention on Human Rights, which provides that: 'everyone has the right to respect for his private and family life, his home and his correspondence.'

Telephone calls made from business premises may be covered by notions of 'private life' and 'correspondence' within the meaning of Article 8. The argument of the UK Government that an employer should in principle, without the prior knowledge of the employee, be able to monitor calls made by the employee on telephones provided by the employer, could not be accepted.

As no warning had been given to the applicant that calls made on the telephones in her office at Merseyside Police Headquarters would be liable to interception, she would have had a reasonable expectation of privacy for such calls. Therefore, Article 8 was applicable.

There was a reasonable likelihood that calls made by the applicant from her office were intercepted by the Merseyside Police with the primary aim of gathering material to assist in the defence of sex discrimination proceedings brought against them. This constituted an 'interference by a public authority' within the meaning of Article 8(2), with the exercise of the applicant's right to respect for her private life and correspondence.

Telephone conversations made from home are covered by the notions of 'private life' and 'correspondence' within the meaning of Article 8 of the Convention.

However, there was insufficient evidence in the present case to amount to a 'reasonable likelihood' that the applicant's calls at home had actually been intercepted. Therefore, no violation of Article 8 with regard to telephone calls made from the applicant's home was established.

That the applicant was unable to seek relief at national level in relation to her complaint concerning her office telephones was a violation of Article 13 of the Convention, which provides: 'Everyone whose rights and freedoms as set forth in this Convention are violated shall have an effective remedy before a national authority notwithstanding that the violation has been committed by persons acting in an official capacity.'

Article 13 requires the provision of a remedy at national level allowing the competent domestic authority both to deal with the substance of the relevant Convention complaint and to grant appropriate relief. However, such a remedy is only required in respect of grievances which can be regarded as 'arguable' in terms of the Convention.

In the present case, the applicant had an arguable claim that calls made from her office telephones were intercepted and that this amounted to a violation of Article 8. Since there was no provision in domestic law to regulate internal communications systems operated by public authorities, such as the Merseyside Police, she was unable to seek relief at national level.

The evidence adduced by the applicant in support of her complaint that calls made from her home telephone were intercepted was not sufficient to found an arguable claim within the meaning of Article 13 of a violation so as to entitle her to an effective remedy at national level.

An award of £10,600 compensation would be made. £10,000 was a just and equitable amount of compensation for non-pecuniary loss. The interception of calls made on her office telephone was a serious infringement of the applicant's rights, bearing in mind that it appeared to have been carried out by the police with the primary purpose of gathering material to be used against her in sex discrimination proceedings. A further £600 would be awarded as reimbursement of the applicant's personal expenses incurred in attending the hearing before the Court.

In contrast, random monitoring of patients' telephone calls at two special hospitals – Rampton and Ashworth, was held to be a legitimate interference with patients' rights under Article 8 as 'it went no further than was strictly necessary to achieve the permitted aim' – *R* v *(1) Ashworth Special Hospital Authority (2) Secretary of State for Health ex parte N* [2001].

In this case the hospital was subject to special regulations under the Mental Health Act 1983 (Directions) which gave the authorities discretionary powers to record and subsequently listen to a random 10 per cent of the outgoing and incoming calls of patients. Calls subject to legal professional privilege (i.e. between lawyer and patient) were not recorded or listened to.

A risk assessment had been completed which led management to identify the need to monitor and listen to calls because the hospital contained high risk patients.

On judicial review the High Court found that even though the patient in question was not high risk, there was a significant risk to patients, staff and members of the public and that random monitoring of any patient's calls on the basis of choosing a random 10 per cent was justifiable and went no further than was strictly necessary to achieve their permitted purpose – to discharge their statutory duties under the Mental Health Act. To do this and to ensure that both treatment and security were safeguarded, interference with the patient's rights under Article 8 was permissible.

In this case the patient, C, was within the category of patients who were dangerous and violent and had criminal propensities. Random monitoring would achieve the legitimate security aim and the hospital had established the existence of a compelling need for the measure which was proportionate to the aim to be achieved.

It is clear that most employers would not be able to justify such monitoring!

MISUSE OF PRIVATE DETECTIVES - BREACH OF ARTICLE 8

What happens to evidence collected by private detectives unlawfully, for example, they trick their way into an employee's house posing as someone else and take a video in a hidden camera? The Court of Appeal ruled on this very point in a claim by Jean Jones against her employers, the University of Warwick, when she was on sick leave and suing them for an alleged disability.

In *Jones* v *University of Warwick* [2003] 3 All ER 760 CA, the Court of Appeal considered whether a defendant to a personal injury claim would be allowed to use as evidence a video of the claimant that was obtained by filming the claimant in her home without her knowledge after the person taking the film had obtained access to the claimant's home by deception.

The original district judge had ruled that the defendant to a personal injury claim (University of Warwick) could not rely on a video film of the claimant (Jean Jones) recorded without her knowledge.

The claimant was employed by the defendant. She had dropped a cash box onto her wrist at work. She alleged significant continuing disability and claimed substantial special damages. The defendant admitted liability but contended that the claimant had virtually recovered and had no significant ongoing disability.

An enquiry agent, acting for the defendant's insurers, obtained access to the claimant's home by posing as a market researcher and filmed the claimant using a hidden camera. The film was disclosed to the claimant.

The district judge had ordered the evidence to be excluded on the basis that the court should not give any approval to the defendant's agent's improper method of gaining entry into the claimant's home. The judge on appeal reversed that decision on the basis that the overriding objective was to deal with a case justly and that the claimant should be prevented from making an inflated or exaggerated claim if there was evidence to contravert it.

The Court of Appeal held that:

> *After the coming into force of the Human Rights Act 1998 the court recognised that there were competing public interests that had to be reconciled as far as possible.*
>
> *The fact that the defendant's insurers had been responsible for the trespass involved in entering the claimant's house and infringing her privacy contrary to Art.8 European Convention on Human Rights was a relevant circumstance for the court to weigh in the balance when coming to a decision as to how it should properly exercise its discretion in making orders as to the management of the proceedings under CPR 1.1 and CPR 32.1.*
>
> *The Convention did not decide what was to be the consequence of evidence being obtained in breach of Art.8. That was a matter for the domestic court and if it could be said to have breached Art.8(1) by making the order that it had decided the law required in accordance with CPR 1.1 and CPR 32.1 it would be acting within Art.8(2) in doing so.*
>
> *This was not a case where the conduct of the defendant's insurers was so outrageous that the defence should be struck out.*
>
> *Therefore the case had to be tried and it would be artificial and undesirable for the actual evidence that was relevant not to be placed before the judge who was trying the case. To exclude the evidence would create a wholly undesirable situation. Therefore it would not be right to interfere with the judge's decision not to exclude it.*
>
> *While not excluding the evidence, it was appropriate to make clear that the conduct of the insurers was improper and unjustified. For that*

reason, subject to further argument, the defendant should pay the costs of the proceedings to resolve the issue of admissibility.

Employers in the public sector are able to be sued directly under the Human Rights Act 1998 but employees in the private sector cannot sue directly under the Act.

HUMAN RIGHTS ASPECTS OF TRIALS AND TRIBUNALS

Since the courts and Employment Tribunals are in the public sector they are legally obliged to consider human rights' aspects in any criminal or civil trial.

In *De Keyser Ltd* v *Wilson* [2001] IRLR 324, Miss Wilson had brought several claims in the Employment Tribunal including a claim for work-related stress. Her employers' representative had sent a letter of instruction to a psychiatrist, to examine her for the purposes of the proceedings but had written an entirely improper and biased set of instructions to the expert. After this letter was disclosed at the directions hearing , the regional chairman decided, of his own motion, to hold a hearing to determine whether or not the employers' notice of appearance should be struck out under rule 13(2) of the Employment Tribunal's rules of procedure.

At that hearing, the tribunal concluded that the letter of instruction to the medical specialist contained material which was irrelevant and abusive. It decided to exercise its discretion and ordered that the employers' notice of appearance be struck out on the ground that the proceedings had been conducted in a scandalous manner and in breach of the Human Rights Act 1998. The employers appealed against that decision.

The EAT overturned the decision to strike out and held:

The employment tribunal had erred in exercising its discretion to strike out the employers' notice of appearance on the ground that the manner in which they had conducted the proceedings had been scandalous in terms of rule 13(2)(e) of the Employment Tribunals Rules of Procedure and in breach of the Human Rights Act 1998.

The employment tribunal erred in taking into account that there was irrelevant and abusive material in a letter instructing a medical expert to examine the applicant in order to establish whether her claim that she had a depressive illness brought on by work-related stress was well founded.

So long as the applicant persisted with a complaint that she suffered stress or other ill health by reason of the employers' actions or actions for which the employers were responsible, she could expect to be required to submit herself for relevant and appropriate medical examination.

An examination in such circumstances did not infringe any human right. Her right to privacy was in opposition to, and needed to be qualified only so far as necessary by, the right of both parties to have a just trial of the issues between them.

The fact that one doctor had been instructed in a manner which gave great offence at several levels did not preclude the later and correct instruction of another doctor.

The tribunal had it well within its power that there should be no examination of the applicant by the doctor to whom the offensive instruction had been given and no offensive instruction of some other doctor.

The tribunal had also erred in failing to ask whether a fair trial of the issues was still possible notwithstanding the letter of instruction. In a case not involving deliberate disobedience or failure to perform an order of the court, whether a fair trial is still possible is a crucial factor in relation to a discretion to strike out the whole of a case.

Since there was no doubt that a fair trial was still possible, even if the instruction letter was scandalous, a striking out was entirely disproportionate and the tribunal's order would therefore be set aside.

The employment tribunal had also erred in holding that references to aspects of the applicant's personal life in the letter of instruction to the medical expert amounted to a breach of her right to respect for her private and family life under Article 8 of Schedule 1 to the Human Rights Act 1998.

It was impossible to discern any actionable breach of Article 8. No public authority was concerned, none of the material was confidential and the recipient doctor would have been bound by conventional medical confidence. The letter of instruction was to be seen by the applicant's solicitors and she was free to resist its being acted on in the sense of its leading to a requirement upon her to attend for examination.

Seeking medical reports in litigation is not a breach of human rights.

Just as an aside it has been unsuccessfully argued that seeking disclosure of medical records and requiring medical examinations may be a breach of that person's rights under Article 8.

Because of the data subject's rights under the Data Protection Act 1998 to give their express consent for disclosure of sensitive data (under s.2) which includes health data, a court or tribunal cannot 'order' the disclosure of medical records or reports. Their powers are limited to ordering the claimant to give their consent to disclosure.

If the claimant refuses, then the court or tribunal has the power to strike out their claim. But is that a breach of the individual's Article 8 rights?

This is what happened in the case of *Hanlon* v *Kirklees Borough Council* EAT UKEAT/0119/04/ILB & UKEAT/0120/04/ILB. Mr Hanlon sued his employers for disability discrimination and was ordered to give his consent to the disclosure of all relevant medical records. He refused to give his consent so the Employment Tribunal Chairman struck out his claim.

Mr Hanlon appealed to the EAT claiming that the action of the Tribunal Chairman was a breach of his right to respect for privacy.

But as the EAT held there always has to be a balancing act between protecting an individual's right to respect for their privacy – in this case refusing to disclose his medical records – and the right of the defendant to know the case against him and to have all relevant documents disclosed to him.

The EAT dismissed his appeal, saying that:

> *[There is no] absolute right of privacy but it is subject to a protection and rights of others and it seems to me that the balancing exercise which was clearly performed by both Chairmen clearly balances up the right for privacy as regards medical records with the proper conduct of the litigation in this case and I am satisfied that no human rights Articles were unfairly breached.*

TAPPING COMPANY TELEPHONES

Tapping telephones on company property, as we have seen, does not offend Regulation of Investigatory Powers Act 2000 or The Telecommunications (Lawful Business Practice) (Interception Of Communications) Regulations 2000 (the 'Lawful Business Regulations') since this is regarded as a 'private system' and therefore belongs to the employer which he is entitled to monitor.

INTERCEPTIONS AUTHORISED UNDER THE LAWFUL BUSINESS PRACTICE REGULATIONS

The regulations authorize businesses to monitor or record communications on their telecoms systems *without consent* for the following purposes:

a) To establish the existence of facts relevant to the business.

For example, keeping records of transactions and other communications in cases where it is necessary or desirable to know the specific facts of the conversation.

b) To ascertain compliance with regulatory or self-regulatory practices or procedures relevant to the business.

For example, monitoring as a means to check that the business is complying with regulatory or self-regulatory rules or guidelines.

c) To ascertain or demonstrate standards which are or ought to be achieved by persons using the telecoms system.

For example, monitoring for purposes of quality control or staff training.

d) To prevent or detect crime.

For example, monitoring or recording to detect fraud or corruption, if an employer suspected that an employee was disclosing confidential information.

e) To investigate or detect the unauthorised use of their telecoms systems.

For example, monitoring to ensure that employees do not breach company rules regarding use of the telecoms system.

f) To ensure the effective operation of the system.

For example, monitoring for viruses or other threats to the system; automated processes such as caching or load distribution.

The regulations also authorise businesses to monitor (but not record) without consent in the following cases:

g) For the purpose of determining whether or not they are communications relevant to the business.

For example, checking email accounts to access business communications in staff absence.

h) In the case of communications to a confidential anonymous counselling or support helpline.

For example, monitoring calls to confidential, welfare helplines in order to protect or support helpline staff.

REQUIREMENT TO INFORM STAFF OF INTERCEPTIONS MADE UNDER THE REGULATION

If businesses intend to make interceptions without consent for the purposes authorised under the regulations, they are required to 'make all reasonable efforts to inform every person who may use their telecoms system that communications may be intercepted' (Resolution 3).

Employers could amend their contracts of employment or staff handbook and place this information on email and the intranet informing staff that interceptions may take place.

The persons who use a system are the people who make direct use of it. Someone who calls from outside, or who receives a call outside, using another system is not a user of the system on which the interception is made. So clients or third parties who send emails do not have to be notified that their emails may be intercepted or read.

INTERCEPTIONS OUTSIDE THE SCOPE OF THE REGULATIONS

If businesses wish to make interceptions for purposes outside the scope of the regulations, they will need to gain consent of the sender and the intended recipient of the communication.

For example, Interceptions for purposes such as marketing or market research; or interceptions for any other purposes that fall outside the list in Section 3 above.

GAINING CONSENT FOR AN INTERCEPTION OUTSIDE THE SCOPE OF THE REGULATIONS

The Regulation of Investigatory Powers Act authorizes interceptions in cases where the interceptor has reasonable grounds to believe that he has the consent of both the sender and the intended recipient of the communication.

If businesses need to intercept communications for purposes outside the scope of the regulations, they could take a number of steps to ensure that they gain the consent of staff and third parties:

- Employers could insert a clause in employment contracts by which employees consent to calls being monitored or recorded.
- The telephone operator or receptionist could ask third parties at the start of a call whether they consented to their call being monitored or recorded.
- A call could start with a recorded message stating that calls might be monitored or recorded unless outsiders requested otherwise.

At a minimum, an employer would need to give outside callers an opportunity to refuse consent to interception and to be able to continue with the call.

DATA PROTECTION ACT IMPLICATIONS

Anybody who intercepts a communication will need to be sure that their actions are authorised under the Regulation of Investigatory Powers Act and comply with the requirements of the Data Protection Act 1998.

The Lawful Business Practice Regulations make an exception to the rule established in the Regulation of Investigatory Powers Act that consent is needed before an interception can take place. If a business intercepted a communication in accordance with the regulations, it would not risk civil liability under the Regulation of Investigatory Powers Act for unlawful interception.

However, employers should be aware that any interception which involves obtaining, recording or otherwise processing personal data by means of automated equipment (for example recording calls or monitoring and reading emails) also falls within the scope of the Data Protection Act 1998. So too does the holding or processing of personal data after the interception has taken place.

MODEL CLAUSES

PRECEDENT 1

Rules about using company property such as fax, post and correspondence generally.

1. Using company facilities

It is strictly forbidden to use the company facilities such as use of photocopier, company stationery, mail or courier services, franking facility, telephones or any other company machinery or equipment for private use. This includes sending and receiving emails and using the Internet for private use which is strictly forbidden.

2. Correspondence coming to the office

The company reserves the right to open all correspondence that is sent to the company whether addressed to an individual or not, other than if the envelope is clearly marked 'Strictly Private and Confidential - This is to be opened by addressee only'.

3. Correspondence or parcels in special circumstances

Where any abuse of this policy is suspected or where unauthorised or illegal activity is suspected or there is any suspicion of the package being from a terrorist or action group designed to cause physical harm, then any item of correspondence whether marked personal or not may be confiscated and may be opened.

If anyone is found to be using the company facilities for their own or others use which is not related to company business, then disciplinary action will be taken which may include summary dismissal.

4. In staff's absence

Please note that when a member of staff is absent, another, duly authorised member of staff may open any business correspondence or packages that are sent to the company, other than where the item is marked, for example, Strictly Private. Emails may also be opened in order to ensure that company business continues uninterrupted during that person's absence.

CHAPTER 9

Pre-Employment Checks and References

PRE-EMPLOYMENT CHECKS

CHECKING QUALIFICATIONS AND SIMILAR

There have been cases over the years of individuals being employed in senior and sometimes professional jobs such as doctors where no proper checks have been made as to their educational and professional qualifications – and they have turned out to be bogus!

In August 2005, it was reported in *The Times* (19 August 2005) that a 'Hospital Chief had forged his degree' in order to obtain the Chief Executive post when two health authorities merged to form the Shrewsbury and Telford Hospitals NHS Trust. Neil Taylor had been embarrassed at his lack of formal post-school qualifications and so had forged a first-class honours degree. It was only when his CV was checked and he initially refused to produce evidence of his BA in Business Administration and Economics from Nottingham University, that the eventual degree certificate was produced and revealed to be a fake.

Taylor was charged with the criminal offence of theft – obtaining a pecuniary advantage by deception and attempting to commit the same offence.

In *R* v *Callender* [1992] 3 All ER 51, Mr Callender agreed to prepare accounts for a number of small businessmen, having falsely held himself out as being professionally qualified. He was convicted under s16(2)(c) of the Theft Act 1968. It was held that 'employment' covered a contract for services, and therefore covered self-employed people who hired out their services in this way.

In the financial services sector it is common practice to require job candidates to bring with them to their interviews the originals of their educational qualifications. The following example is typical of a clause in a letter inviting the candidate to an interview:

'When you attend for your interview you should bring with you the original certificates of your educational and professional qualifications. Please do not bring copies and please do not send the originals through the post.

In any case where you cannot locate the originals of your certificates, we reserve the right with your consent to telephone and verify your qualifications with the relevant establishment.

In the event that you start in our employment and it is then discovered that there is any ambiguity or falsehood associated with what you have reported that you have obtained by way of examinations and professional qualifications, we reserve the right to terminate your employment summarily, that is, without notice or pay in lieu on the grounds of gross misconduct.'

CHECKING CREDIT

Employers in the financial services sector often also check credit ratings for individuals for specific posts, for example, trading, as those individuals are not permitted to have an overdraft or have been in arrears of mortgage payments or in debt on credit cards. The rationale for such strict rules is clear – in managing other people's money, they must be able to manage their own financial affairs with the utmost probity and transparency. Confidence would be lost in someone trading with private client or corporate funds if that individual was unable to manage their own financial affairs.

It is also a rule for some individuals in clearing banks that they do not have an overdraft – for similar reasons of probity and security.

There is nothing unlawful about a prospective employer checking a job applicant's credit history as long as the individual has given their informed consent and understands the reasons for the request.

The employer, the data controller, for his part, must comply with all the principles of the Data Protection Act 1998 including telling the credit reference agency the use to which the data will be put. The data should only be kept as long as is necessary and should be checked to ensure that it is correct.

FOOTPRINTS

Any credit check results in what is known as a 'footprint' being left with credit reference agencies, such as Experian, Credit Expert and Equifax. If a large number of footprints appear on a record, it can have a detrimental effect on that individual's credit rating.

Prospective employers should therefore advise job applicants of this to ensure that they are committed to their application for the job before they go through the application process.

AGENCIES WHICH CHECK ON TEMPS AND CONTRACTORS

In the contracting sector it is often the case that a contractor may obtain work through an agency or headhunter. The agency or headhunter may conduct credit or other checks before taking the contractor on their books or putting them forward to a client. It is essential for the client or 'end user' to be sure that references and checks have been done before the individual is put forward for consideration or for interview. This is a matter that should properly be dealt with in the terms of business between the agency or recruitment consultancy and the client.

There is an interesting question as to whether if the agency did not conduct credit and other checks, this would be a breach of the Conduct of Employment Agencies and Employment Businesses Regulations 2003.

Regulation 18(d) requires contract agencies not to introduce a work-seeker to a hirer until the agency:

> *has obtained sufficient information from the hirer to select a suitable work-seeker for the position which the hirer seeks to fill, including the following information ... the experience, training, qualifications and any authorisation which the hirer considers are necessary ... for a work-seeker to possess in order to work in the position.*

It is possible that the requirement to pass a credit check would be a 'qualification' within the meaning of this regulation because although 'qualification' in the narrow sense can mean a certification by an independent body that particular levels or training and/or experience and/or competence have been attained, in its ordinary meaning it refers more widely to any quality which fits a person for a position.

The introductory words are 'sufficient information ... to select a suitable work-seeker for the position which the hirer seeks to fill'. This would favour a broad interpretation.

So if an agency does wish to conduct a credit rating it must have obtained the information that a credit check was necessary, before introducing the contractor to the client.

Having obtained this information an agency is required by regulation 19(b) not to put the candidate forward without confirming that the candidate has the necessary 'qualifications' - for example, that they would pass the credit check required by the client.

Breach by the agency of regulation 19 is an offence and the agency could be reported to the Department of Trade and Industry (DTI). Prosecution by the DTI is, however, separate from the question of whether an individual would be entitled to bring a civil claim for compensation against the agency. In order to bring a civil claim the individual would need to be able to show that the agency's breach of the regulations had caused monetary loss.

So, for example, it would be crucial for the agency to explain to any candidate that even if a conditional job offer is made, they should not resign from their job or reject any other job offer, until all the checks and references have been verified and confirmed.

A typical clause in an offer letter and contract of employment might read:

> We reserve the right with your informed consent to undertake credit checks on you to ensure that you have no County Court Judgements (CCJs), undeclared maintenance orders under the Child Support Agency (CSA) or Attachment of Earnings Orders. In addition it is a requirement of this particular post that you are not and never have been in arrears with your mortgage or other payments such as credit cards or similar.
>
> If you have had any financial debts or indebtedness, you are required to declare them at interview so that your explanations can be checked. Our continued interest in pursuing your application to work for us will depend upon our credit checks. We therefore invite you to be totally honest with us about your own financial dealings.

Below is an example form for a prospective employer to complete to indicate their consent to credit and other background checks:

In connection with my application for employment with ....(the 'Company'), I hereby agree as follows:

1. General consent to background investigation.

As a condition of Company's consideration of my employment application, I give permission to Company to investigate my personal and employment history. I understand that this background investigation will include, but not be limited to, verification of all information on my employment application.

2. Consent to contact past employers.

I specifically give permission to Company to contact all of my prior employers for references. I further give permission to all current or previous employers and/or managers or supervisors to discuss my relevant personal and employment history with Company, consent to the release of such information orally or in writing, and hereby release them from all liability and agree not to sue them for defamation or other claims based upon any statements they make to any representative of Company. I further agree to indemnify all past employers for any liability they may incur because of their reliance upon this agreement.

3. Consent to contact government departments and other agencies.

I further give permission to the Company to receive a copy of any information obtained in the file of any court or government department or any other relevant agency concerning or relating to me.

I understand that the scope of this investigation will be limited to whatever the applicable law provides.

4. Cooperation with investigation.

I agree to fully cooperate in Company's background investigation and to give whatever reasonable consents are required by any government department or agency.

REFERENCES

The law concerning references is often misunderstood by employers. Some employers still believe that they can only give a 'good' reference. This is not the case. The reference has to be 'honest and accurate'.

It is common practice for employers to require at least two references from previous employers, at least one being from the current employer.

OFFER OR INVITATION TO TREAT?

Many, if not most offers of employment contain conditions that must be satisfied before the offer can be accepted, or if accepted, for employment to continue. The offer letter should make it clear whether at the first stage this is merely an 'invitation to treat' rather than an offer.

An offer is an expression of willingness to contract made with the intention that it shall become binding on the offeror as soon as it is accepted by the offeree. An invitation to treat is not an offer – it is merely an invitation to others to make offers. It follows that an invitation to treat cannot be accepted in such a way as to form a contract and equally the person extending the invitation is not bound to accept any offers made to them.

Thus a letter sent to a prospective candidate stating that the employer was very pleased to have met the individual and that if the individual would indicate whether they would be willing to put themselves forward as the candidate for the post, once the conditions had been met, for example, by satisfactory references, medical screening, and so on, the employer would then be willing to accept the individual's offer to join their employment.

An example of a common situation involving an invitation to treat is the display of goods with a price ticket in a shop window. The goods are not being offered for sale at that price on the price tag. Members of the public are being invited to make an offer to buy those goods at that price. If the shopkeeper declines to sell at that price, no contract has been formed and therefore there has been no breach of contract by the shopkeeper.

The classic case on this point is *Fisher* v *Bell* [1960] 3 All ER 731, in which a Bristol shopkeeper was prosecuted for offering offensive weapons for sale, by having flick-knives on display in his window. It was held that the shopkeeper was not guilty as the display in the shop window was not an offer for sale but only an invitation to treat.

A statement of intention is also incapable of forming the basis of a contract, even though the party to whom it was made acts on it. Examples include cases involving letters of comfort, where parent companies state their present intention to support their subsidiaries, but subsequently fail to accept responsibility for the debts of those subsidiaries (see *Kleinwort Benson* v *Malaysian Mining Corporation* [1989] 1 All ER 785).

Offer letters need to make clear whether the prospective candidate is being asked to offer themselves for the position – in which case if the conditions are all met, the employer will accept the offer put forward by the job candidate. Before this stage is reached the candidate should be warned not to resign from their current employment.

SATISFACTORY REFERENCES

It is common wording to see offers of employment 'subject to satisfactory references'. The problem is to whose satisfaction do those references have to be ?

In *Wishart* v *National Association of Citizens' Advice Bureaux* [1990] IRLR 393, that question had to be determined by the Court of Appeal.

Mr Wishart applied for a post as an information officer with responsibility for welfare rights in the defendants' information production group. He was offered the post 'subject to the receipt of satisfactory written references'. His sickness absence record in his previous employment was significantly high. NACAB decided not to confirm the offer on the basis of the sickness absence history disclosed by the previous employer.

Mr Wishart sued for breach of contract.

The Court of Appeal held that the word 'satisfactory' in this context had to mean satisfactory to the employer concerned, that is, it had a subjective meaning, rather than as Mr Wishart argued, satisfactory to any objective employer.

The court held that:

> *Where an offer of employment is conditional upon 'satisfactory' references being furnished, that is likely to have a subjective meaning of 'satisfactory' to the defendants.*
>
> *It is highly probable that no objective test is applicable and that there is no obligation in law upon the employer in considering the references other than to consider in good faith whether they were satisfactory to them.*
>
> *The natural reading of a communication, the purpose of which is to tell the prospective employee that part of the decision on whether he*

is firmly offered the post has yet to be made, is that the employer is reserving the right to make up his own mind when the references have been received and studied.

Although it is possible for an employer to make an offer conditional on something to be objectively determined (for example, the passing of a medical examination), it was very hard to see that the defendants' letter in the present case fell into that category.

Therefore, it was unlikely that the plaintiff would be able to show that the test was objective in the sense that a reasonable person in the position of the defendants, with the particular post to fill, would not regard the references as a satisfactory basis on which to appoint the plaintiff.

VICARIOUS LIABILITY FOR CRIMINAL ACTS

What is the position of an employer who does not take up references when they are employing someone in a position of trust? Could the employer be held liable for the criminal acts committed by that member of staff under the principle of vicarious liability? The answer is 'Yes'.

In *Nahhas* v *Pier House Management (Cheyne Walk) Ltd* [1984] TLR 10 February 1984, a tenant brought a claim against the apartment managers and an estate agent for £23 250 for jewellery stolen from her flat by a porter employed by the apartment managers.

They had recruited a porter without checking his references. Had they done so they would have discovered he had had numerous convictions for theft and larceny. He had access to the tenants' keys and walked into the plaintiff's flat one day and stole her jewellery. Her household contents policy would not pay out any compensation as there had been no break-in.

Ms Nahhas sued the porter's employers on the basis that their negligent recruitment procedure had led directly to her loss and they should be held vicariously liable for his criminal act.

The High Court agreed. They held that:

The Apartment Managers were vicariously liable for fraud of their employee committed in the course of his employment and in breach of manager's duty to protect the plaintiff's flat. They had further been negligent in job recruitment procedures.

DUTY TO GIVE REFERENCES?

Apart from specific regulations about the giving of references and their content under the Financial Services Authority, there is no legal obligation on any employer to provide a reference on behalf of an employee. However, there may be some 'moral duty' according to the Court of Appeal in *Spring* v *Guardian Assurance plc* [1993] IRLR 122. Here the President of the Court of Appeal stated that:

> *Other employers ... are commonly thought to be under a moral or social duty to do so if a reference is requested by either the employee or the prospective employer. If, however, a former employer declines to give a reference, this may almost be as damaging to the employee as an unsatisfactory reference.*

GENERAL RULES ABOUT REFERENCES

However once a reference is given, it must be accurate and honest and not misleading. When employers do provide references, they must take care to be as accurate as possible and to present a full picture of employees and their work.

In *Bartholomew* v *London Borough of Hackney* [1999] IRLR 246, the Court of Appeal dismissed Mr Bartholomew's claim that by including the circumstances of his leaving, his employers were in breach of their duty of care to him, albeit the reference was accurate, but he claimed the reference was 'unfair'.

In this case Mr Bartholomew had been suspended on suspicion of fraud and disciplinary proceedings had started against him. As a compromise to his racial discrimination proceedings, Hackney agreed a voluntary severance package and withdrew the disciplinary charges. However, when the London Borough of Richmond requested a reference, the reference stated that he had taken voluntary severance following the deletion of his post and that, at the time of leaving, he 'was suspended from work due to a charge of gross misconduct and disciplinary action had commenced. This disciplinary action lapsed automatically on his departure from the authority.'

The Court of Appeal held that:

> *An employer is under a duty of care to provide a reference which is in substance true, accurate and fair. The reference must not give an unfair or misleading impression overall, even if its discrete components are factually correct. However, the duty of care owed by an ex-employer to an ex-employee in accordance with Spring v Guardian Assurance plc*

[1994] IRLR 460 does not mean that a reference must in every case be full and comprehensive.

In the present case, though the form of the reference might have been improved upon in some respects, it was not as a whole unfair, inaccurate and false. Had the defendants omitted all reference to the suspension, they might have considered themselves as failing in their duty not to be unfair or misleading to the recipient of the reference.

In *Kidd* v *AXA Equity and Law Life Assurance Society plc* [2000] IRLR 301, Mr Kidd complained that he had lost a job offer with Allied Dunbar because of the reference his former employers had given about him. He argued that the reference supplied by Equity and Law (E & L), in the form of an industry questionnaire plus two letters, made mention of the fact that they had received complaints about Mr Kidd from clients, that investigations into those complaints were not yet completed but it had been deemed necessary to carry out a customer-care exercise and interview a number of other clients who to date had not complained.

Mr Kidd made a claim against E & L for damages on the ground that they had a duty of care to provide him with a reference making full and frank disclosure of all relevant matters and to ensure that the reference was fair and not misleading, and that they were in breach of such a duty.

Reference was also made to the review of Mr Kidd's business required by Lautro (the former regulatory body and forerunner of the Financial Services Authority). E & L gave no answer to the question relating to the honesty of the claimant.

Mr Kidd argued that the reference should have made clear that Lautro's disquiet related to a package devised and promoted by the company and sold under its direction, and that the complaints by clients had not yet been thoroughly investigated. He also argued that the reference should have made mention of the fact that Mr Kidd had not been interviewed in relation to those complaints, that he disputed the allegations, that he had not properly explained certain aspects of the equity release package to the clients and that the clients concerned had solicitors to advise them in respect of the matter. The reference should also have contained details of his sales record. In other words, the reference was incomplete and gravely misleading.

The High Court ruled that:

The defendants did not have a duty of care to give the claimant a reference which was fair, full and comprehensive. The duty owed by the giver of a reference to the subject of that reference, whether arising in tort or from contract, is a duty to take reasonable care not to give misleading information about him, whether as a result of the unfairly selective provision of information, or by the inclusion of facts and opinions in such a manner as to give rise to a false or mistaken inference in the mind of a reasonable recipient.

The giver of a reference owes no additional duty to the subject to take reasonable care to give a full and comprehensive reference, or to include in a reference all material facts.

The nature and extent of such a duty and of any breach would be extremely difficult to formulate and define. Moreover, imposing an obligation on employers to give employees a full, frank and comprehensive reference was not necessary in the public interest nor in the interests of employees since such a reference would have to include the bad as well as the good.

The reference provided by the defendants in respect of the claimant did not amount to a breach of the duty to take care not to provide misleading information.

To prove a breach of that duty, a claimant must establish:

(i) that information provided in the reference was misleading;

(ii) that the provision of such misleading information was likely to have a material effect upon the mind of a reasonable recipient of the reference to the detriment of the claimant;

(iii) that the defendants were negligent in providing such reference.

In the present case, the information supplied by the defendants was not misleading, materially or at all, and was not negligently provided.

However, in both *Spring's* case (*Spring* v *Guardian Assurance plc* [1994] IRLR 460 HL and in *Cox* v *Sun Alliance Life Ltd* [2001] IRLR 448 references were provided that suggested that both claimants had been dishonest.

In *Spring's* case the reference stated that 'he was a man of little or no integrity and could not be trusted'. Whilst Judge Lever QC in the High Court [1992] IRLR 173, determined that Mr Spring 'may have been a fool, he was not a rogue'. Spring's counsel described the reference in the context of the insurance industry as 'the kiss of death'.

In *Cox's* case, the Court of Appeal focused on the content of the reference where an employee has resigned while under investigation.

The employers were found liable in negligence for failing to take reasonable care to be accurate and fair when they provided a reference which suggested that they had a reasonable basis for dismissing the claimant on the ground of dishonesty amounting to corruption. In fact, the charges of dishonesty had never been put to him, had not been made the subject of proper investigation and disciplinary proceedings were shelved pending negotiations of a settlement.

Lord Justice Mummery held that the discharge of the duty of care to provide an accurate and fair reference will usually involve making 'reasonable inquiry into the factual basis of the statements in the reference'. In order to take reasonable care, according to Lord Justice Mummery:

> *An employer should confine unfavourable statements about an employee to those matters into which they had made reasonable investigation and had reasonable grounds for believing to be true. Where the employee has resigned, there is no obligation to continue with an investigation into the employee's conduct. But if an investigation is discontinued, the employer should confine its unfavourable comments to matters which had been investigated before the resignation.*

He helpfully added that, in order to avoid 'costly litigation' about references:

> *In a case where the terms of an agreed resignation or of the compromise of an unfair dismissal claim make provision for the supply of a reference, the parties should ensure as far as possible that the exact wording of a fair and accurate reference is fully discussed, clearly agreed and carefully recorded in writing in COT3 at the same time as other severance terms.*

AGREED WORDING IN COMPROMISE AGREEMENTS

A common form of wording about agreed references in compromise agreements includes the following:

> *The Company agrees that on receipt of a request for a reference by any actual or prospective new employer of the Employee (provided that such reference whether oral or in writing is addressed to the Manager of Human Resources,......................................) the Company will provide (except as set out below), in respect of the Employee, a reference on the Employee's behalf in the terms of Annex 1 hereto and will respond to oral requests for such a reference in a manner which is consistent with the terms and spirit of the agreed draft, subject always to the Company's compliance with its obligations to third parties relating to the giving of references and provided that no information comes to*

light after the execution of this compromise agreement which gives the Company any reason to doubt any of the matters set out in Annex 1. Also the agreed reference will not be given if any actual or prospective new employer of the Employee requests a reference from the Company and the Company is, in respect of that request, required to comply with the FSA rules for the time being in force or, as the case may be, the rules for the time being in force of any other body by which the Company may for the time being be regulated at any time hereafter. In such a case, the Company will notify the employee of this new condition and the Company will then be free to respond to the reference request in such manner as the Company in its entire discretion considers appropriate.

NO NEGATIVE INFERENCE

Some employers will only provide confirmation of employment dates and job title. In such case there is normally a clear notice that nothing of a negative inference should be drawn from such a summary form reference.

It is normal to see wording such as this:

It is not the policy of the Bank to provide any further information for references. This does not imply any comment, positive or negative about the employee or the course of employment with the Bank.

FSA RULES

The obligations on employers who are regulated by the Financial Services Authority (FSA) – (a 'regulated employer') – start at the time of recruitment because, if the regulated employer wishes to employ an individual to carry out a 'controlled function', or that individual is a senior manager having significant influence, then approved person status must be obtained.

The regulated employer cannot permit that individual to carry out any of those controlled functions until they have been approved as 'fit and proper' for that purpose by the FSA.

The application for approved person status is made on Form A, which requires a considerable amount of information. It is the responsibility of the prospective employer to submit the application, and reckless submission of inaccurate or misleading information is a criminal offence.

Wide-ranging checks are needed pre-employment. These have to be explained to the prospective employee and specific written consent should be obtained from the employee to ensure compliance with the Data Protection

Code (the Code) and to allow the employer to undertake various credit checks, court proceedings and criminal checks. The only way that an employer can obtain details of all past convictions, including 'spent convictions', is to require the employee to make a joint request with the employer to the Criminal Records Bureau.

'Spent convictions' are those which are normally disregarded after a period of time if no further offences have been committed, under the Rehabilitation of Offenders Act 1974. However there are several exemption orders, exempting various professional employees such as doctors, nurses, accountants, anyone working with children, including the exemption of those who need approved status under the FSA.

References also need to be obtained from previous employers. Some financial institutions have developed a standard form of questionnaire that usually follows directly the questions on the FSA Form A application itself.

These include:

- A full 5 year employment history.
- A determination of fitness and propriety including criminal checks and credit reference enquiries with specific reference to any convictions for fraud, dishonesty, theft, false accounting, perverting the course of justice and so on.
- Reason for leaving, for example, resignation, redundancy, retirement, dismissal, other.
- Financial history including whether the individual has been the subject of any civil proceedings, bankruptcy proceedings, indebtedness to former employer of more than £1000.
- Other information relating to any acts of misconduct for which he may have been investigated, whether he has been the subject of any other investigations including being de-registered or disqualified under the FSA or any other body.

DATA PROTECTION

Part 1 of the Data Protection Code deals with recruitment and selection and obliges employers to tailor their investigations into a candidate's personal data and to be 'proportionate and necessary'. Every search or question must be proportionate and justifiable. Access to sensitive data must be restricted and kept in a secure place.

Although the Code also provides that pre-employment vetting should be limited so far as possible in the case of an approved person, the regulatory requirements will override the guidance in the Code. Once the employee has been recruited, Part 2 of the Data Protection Code makes recommendations for regulating the maintenance of employee records.

One aspect of Financial Services and Markets Act 2000 (FSMA) that directly conflicts with the data protection code of practice, is that the FSA has the right to ask an employer for all spent warnings on an employee's disciplinary record.

DATA SUBJECT RIGHTS OF ACCESS

The writer of the reference may refuse access if requested by the data subject to disclose a reference, but the recipient of a reference may not. So whilst a current employer may refuse to disclose any reference that they have written on an existing employee, a prospective employer who may be the recipient of the reference is obliged to disclose the references it receives to individuals at their request.

However appraisals and reports written on individuals within an organization are not held to be references by the Information Commissioner and individuals automatically have the right to see them.

Information relating to another individual who can be identified by that information (including being identified by the source) may be withheld unless either that third party consents to that disclosure or it is reasonable to redact any information that could identify that third party (S.7 (4) – (6) of the 1998 Act). In rare cases, it may be lawful to supply the information where it identifies a third party, who has not given their consent.

In determining whether it is reasonable to supply information relating to another individual without consent, according to the Code of Practice (Part 2) regard should be had to:

- any duty of confidentiality owed;
- any steps taken by the data controller to seek consent;
- whether the individual is capable of giving consent, that is, whether that individual is still employed or their location known;
- any express refusal of consent.

DIFFERENT TYPES OF REFERENCES

An 'open' reference is one, written and signed by the former employer 'To whom it may concern'. Most employers will not provide open references save in cases where the employer has closed down his business altogether and all the staff are made redundant or where a member of staff wishes to work abroad and needs a written testimonial before obtaining an interview.

Any person providing a reference should note that:

- the author of a reference owes a duty of care to the recipient;
- information given must be accurate and honest, this means not misleading, by omitting detrimental information and recording only positive information;
- state clearly the parameters in which it is given;
- distinguish clearly between statements of fact and statements of opinion;
- only give an opinion on matters within the writer's professional competence;
- It is usual to include the normal disclaimer – *'This reference is given without any legal liability on the part of the Company or the writer of this reference'* –which may not be valid under the Unfair Contract Terms Act 1977 (UCTA).

There is a debate around whether such a disclaimer can be 'reasonable' when the writer of the reference has the facts upon which they are writing and they know that the recipient will normally rely upon that reference when deciding whether or not to confirm any offer of employment. It has been argued that it cannot be reasonable to seek to exclude liability for the accuracy of factual information which the employer possesses.

TO WHOM THE DUTY OF CARE IS OWED

The duty of care on the part of the writer/employer not to make negligent mis-statements in a reference is owed to the recipient and not to the subject of the reference. So held the House of Lords in *Spring's* case. Oral references are subject to the same rules.

AUTOMATED DECISION-MAKING

In some cases decisions which significantly affect the individual are made by computerised programmes, for example, performance at work,creditworthiness and appropriate medical treatment.

If automated decisions are made the data subject must be informed. If an individual objects to processing in this way, the decision must be made by a person.

WORKING WITH EXTERNAL AGENCIES

If an employer provides data to an external agency (for example, an external payroll, service or mailing agency) it is incumbent on the employer to make sure everything is covered by a contract. The external agency is not liable for distress caused by the misuse of data –the data controller is.

Example clause to place at bottom of forms:

> This information will be held and processed for the following purposes
>
> ....
>
> I agree to .... recording and processing this information about me. I understand that this information will be used only for the purpose(s) set out in the statement above, and my consent is conditional upon my employer complying with its duties and obligations under the Data Protection Act.
>
> Signature ....
> Date ....

REFUSAL TO GIVE A REFERENCE

Whilst we have seen that there is no legal duty to provide a reference, (other than under the FSA), it may be deemed to be discriminatory to refuse to provide one.

If the employer's normal policy is to provide references and the reason for refusing to provide a reference in any particular case relates to the fact that the individual concerned had brought discrimination proceedings, then such a denial amounts to an act of victimisation under the Sex Discrimination Act 1975, Race Relations Act 1976 and Disability Discrimination Act 1995 and other anti-discrimination legislation – *Coote* v *Grenada Hospitality Ltd* [1998] IRLR 656 and *Rhys Harper* v *Relaxion Group and ors* [2003] IRLR 484.

However in *Chief Constable of West Yorkshire Police* v *Khan* [2001] IRLR 830 the House of Lords held that the Chief Constable's refusal to provide Detective Sergeant Khan with a reference, after he had left employment, during proceedings that he was bringing for racial discrimination was not an act of victimisation. There was no causal link between not providing a reference during that time and the fact that racial discrimination proceedings had been brought.

Victimisation occurs when, 'in any circumstances relevant for the purposes of any provision of the Act, a person is treated less favourably than others because he has done one of the protected acts'.

The House of Lords held that:

> *In order to determine whether there has been less favourable treatment, the statute calls for a simple comparison between the treatment afforded to the complainant who has done a protected act and the treatment which was or would be afforded to other employees who have not done the protected act.*
>
> *Applying this approach, the applicant in the present case was treated less favourably than other employees in that references were normally provided on request for members of the force seeking new employment.*
>
> *However, the reference was not withheld 'by reason that' the applicant had brought discrimination proceedings, but rather because the employer temporarily needed to preserve his position in the outstanding proceedings.*
>
> *The evidence established that once the litigation had concluded, the request for a reference would have been complied with.*
>
> *Contrary to the view of the Court of Appeal, whether a complainant has been victimised 'by reason' that he has done a protected act is not to be determined by application of a 'but for' test.*
>
> *Employers ought to be able to take steps to preserve their position in pending discrimination proceedings without laying themselves open to a charge of victimisation, and the statute accommodates this approach without any straining of language.*

Lord Nicholls held that:

> *The phrase 'by reason that' does not raise a question of causation as that expression is usually understood. The test is the subjective one of why did the alleged discriminator act as he did? What, consciously or unconsciously, was his reason?*

Lord Hoffmann held:

> *Whether the applicant was treated less favourably 'by reason that' he had brought proceedings raised a question of causation: was the fact that he brought proceedings a reason why he was treated less favourably. It is not enough to say that but for the protected act, the applicant would not have been treated in the way he was.*
>
> *A test which is likely in most cases to give the right answer is to ask whether the employer would have refused the request if the litigation had been concluded, whatever the outcome.*
>
> *If the answer is no, it will usually follow that the reason for the refusal was the existence of the proceedings and not the fact that the employee had commenced them.*
>
> *On the other hand, if the fact that the employee had commenced proceedings under the Act was a real reason why he received less favourable treatment, it is no answer that the employer would have behaved in the same way to an employee who had done some non-protected act such as commencing proceedings otherwise than under the Act.*

Lord Scott held:

> *The language of s.2(1) is not the language of strict causation. The words 'by reason that' suggest that it is the real reason, the core reason, the motive for the treatment complained of that must be identified.*

CLAUSE IN CONTRACT RE CONTINUING OBLIGATION TO REPORT CRIMINAL CHARGES OR REPORTS OF MISCONDUCT TO REGULATORY BODY

REPORTING MISCONDUCT

Due to the nature of the Company's business, it is expected that every member of staff will act with sensitivity, diligence and utmost honesty at all times. Should any matter of concern come to an employee's attention, he/she must report the concern(s) immediately to the Managing Director or any other relevant Board Member. The Company sees it as the duty of every member of staff to report any acts of misconduct (suspected or actual), dishonesty, breach of the Company's rules or breach of any other relevant rules or codes of conduct, committed, contemplated or discussed by any other member of staff or any other third party.

The Company agrees that whatever is reported will be treated with the utmost confidentiality but only insofar as this is practicable.

If any internal or external enquiry or investigation takes place, then any member of staff with any information or knowledge will be expected to cooperate fully. This includes but is not limited to giving information and evidence both written and oral in any investigation, enquiry, judicial process, regulatory investigation, court or employment tribunal proceedings, even after that member of staff has left our employment.

CHAPTER 10

Defamation and the Internet

INTRODUCTION

Employers have a duty not to allow defamatory material to be published on email or the internet. As the publishers of the material, employers may also be liable for such defamation along with the individual who has written the defamatory material as they will be deemed to be disseminating the libellous statements in the course of their employment – for which the employer is also liable.

Key legislation in this area derives from the Defamation Act 1996 and the Information Society Directive (Directive 2001/29/EC). Recent cases are, for example, *Godfrey* v *Demon Internet* [1999] *Journal of Civil Liberties,* 4(2), 260–267 (July), *Dow Jones & Co Inc* v *Gutnick* (2003) *Oxford University Commonwealth Law Journal, Issue 1 Summer 2003, Dow Jones* v *Jameel CA Civ,* [2005] 2 WLR 1614 *and Don King* v *Judd Burstein (Lennox Lewis's New York lawyer)* (2004) Case No: A2/2004/0380. The Court of Appeal has helped to clarify the law in this area.

Amongst other things, they demonstrate that in the context of online defamation:

- It is largely irrelevant where the website is hosted and that what counts is whether the website is accessed in a jurisdiction where the claimant has a reputation capable of being damaged.
- English defamation law can be applied to internet publications irrespective of where the parties are based so long as any such publication cannot be considered negligible and that any action would represent a proportionate and meaningful use of the court's time and resources.
- Internet service providers (ISPs) who fail promptly to remove allegedly defamatory content can themselves become a party to the defamation. They may, in any event, be compelled to disclose details of publishers whose identities are not apparent from the face of any hosted site.

WHAT IS DEFAMATION?

Libel is defamatory written material and can include emails and information posted on the internet. Slander is spoken. A statement would be considered to be defamatory if it:

- 'had the effect of lowering the reputation of the claimant in the estimation of right-thinking members of society generally' (*Sim* v *Stretch* [1936] 52 TLR 671; or
- 'tend to cause others to shun or avoid the claimant' (*Youssoupoff* v *MGM* [1934] 50 TLR 587; *or*
- tend to expose the claimant to 'hatred, contempt or ridicule' (*Parmiter* v *Coupland* [1840] 6 M&W 105.

Defamatory material or libellous statements are those which are untrue and prompted by malice. Both elements have to be proved. Normally malice can be proved by showing that the publisher of the statement knew that the statement was untrue.

DEFENCES

There are a number of defences available to a defendant such as the statement was true, 'qualified privilege', fair comment and justification.

A defendant may, by way of answer, establish that:

- one of the essential elements is absent; or
- the defamatory words are true; or
- some other (several possibilities) reason protects the publication in law. This may be some form of privilege, or innocence;
- a suitable offer of amends has been made.

DEFAMATION ACT 1996

Under the Defamation Act 1996 anyone who is the author, editor or publisher of a defamatory statement is strictly liable, that is, knowledge or intention are not required.

However under s1(1) of the 1996 Act a person has a defence if he can show that:

- he was not the author, editor or publisher;

- he took reasonable care in relation to the publication; and
- he did not know nor had any reason to believe that he had caused or contributed to the publication of a defamatory statement.

LIBEL ON THE NET

The first case concerning libel on the Net was *Godfrey* v *Demon Internet Ltd* LTL 30/3/2000.

Here the claimant, Dr Laurence Godfrey, a lecturer and researcher in physics, brought two libel actions against the defendant, an internet service provider, following two defamatory postings on separate newsgroups owned by the defendant, Demon, who was the then largest English ISP having 90 000 subscribers. One of its services was providing its newsgroups to Usenet newspapers. One of the newsgroups was called 'soc.culture.thai', a discussion group for those interested in the political and cultural affairs of Thailand.

The first posting, for which the first libel action was brought, purported to be by the claimant but was a forgery and was 'squalid, obscene and defamatory'. The second posting, for which the second action was brought, made further allegations of a defamatory nature (see *Laurence Godfrey* v *Demon Internet Ltd* (1999) 4 EMLR 542).

Prior to bringing the actions the claimant had attempted to persuade the defendant to remove the postings from its sites, but without success. The defendant did not dispute the defamatory nature of the postings but claimed that it was not responsible for the material posted by its users on its sites. Upon clarification of the legal position, the defendant changed its procedures.

The defendant agreed to pay damages to the sum of £15 000 and the claimant's costs. It apologised for failing to remove the postings from its servers and for alleging in its defence that the claimant had deliberately provoked them.

Mr Justice Morland held that:

> *ISPs such as Demon were to be treated as publishers for the purposes of English libel law.*

Further:

> *Demon could not rely on the defence under s.1(1) of the Defamation Act 1996 in the period following Dr Godfrey's complaint about the offensive posting on Demon's servers because Demon was put on notice and was required to take reasonable care.*

LESSONS FROM *GODFREY*

Any transmission by email, a website publication and a chat room or bulletin board or newsgroup posting are all publications.

Publication takes place when the image is transmitted and/or placed on the website and publication occurs when a computer generates the message on the server on which the material is stored, on the pc where it was screened and on hard copy downloaded from the website.

The author and the publisher of the material are liable. The publisher includes the website owner, the content provider, the access provider and the employer, vicariously liable for the acts of the employees as a publisher.

The publisher can only successfully defend a claim if he has no actual knowledge of the alleged libel; was not negligent in not knowing of the libel and he did not know or ought to have known that the publication was of a character likely to contain libellous material.

Employers should:

- post notices on the website warning anyone writing material for the website that libellous material is strictly forbidden;
- encourage user ID;
- take steps to exercise editorial control and monitor text and delete unsuitable material;
- take complaints seriously;
- obtain warranties and indemnities from anyone wishing to post notices on the website; and
- take out insurance for legal action.

NORWICH UNION CASE

The dangers of email have been highlighted recently in the first UK case concerning libel by email. Norwich Union was found to have libelled, through its internal email system, a competitor, Western Provident Association (WPA). Norwich Union staff had claimed that the Department of Trade and Industry were investigating WPA and that the group was close to insolvency. Norwich Union paid WPA £450 000 in damages plus costs and gave a public apology.

EMAIL LIBEL

Despite its obvious advantages of speed and convenience, the apparent temporary nature of email can result in the making of unguarded statements, often out of any context.

Although an email can be deleted from the screen, a computer will store copies which may later be recovered and some email systems automatically print out messages for record retention purposes.

If a company enters into litigation in the UK, email messages, unless protected by privilege, will be discoverable in later litigation and therefore must be produced to the other side if they are relevant to the action. The fact that email may only be stored in electronic form does not prevent it being discoverable under English law.

In the Norwich Union case the company was vicariously liable for the defamatory comments of its employees. This may be the case where an employee is acting within the scope of his or her employment even if the act was unauthorised, not for the benefit of the employer (*Lloyd* v *Grace Smith* [1912] AC 716) or expressly forbidden (*Limpus* v *London General Omnibus* [1862] 1 H&C, 526).

The general rule is that any message may be held to be defamatory if on any reasonable basis the message was likely to be available to readers other than the plaintiff. This will include messages sent on the internet and those sent within an internal email system (such as in the Norwich Union case) even if they are addressed to just one person.

PROTECTION FROM LIABILITY

An email may attach privilege in certain circumstances and therefore not be discoverable in subsequent court proceedings.

Where an email is sent through an internal system within a company and is not copied to a third party, qualified privilege may apply. Normal everyday internal communications necessary for the conduct of the business will be protected by qualified privilege so long as no malice is involved. But problems will be caused if email is used for idle gossip.

In the *Norwich Union* case it would appear that the emails in question were not necessary to the conduct of its business as the apology stated that 'Norwich Union deeply regret and sincerely apologise to WPA for the dissemination of the rumours'.

In the light of this case, employees should be made aware of the dangers of email and that serious misuse may result in disciplinary action against the employee. It is important that guidelines on the use and consequences of misuse are circulated to employees not only for education purposes but as a defence if a dismissed employee later claims unfair dismissal.

OTHER CASES

In April 1995 a Police Constable David Eggleton achieved an out-of-court settlement with supermarket chain Asda over a description of him that was circulated between its stores after he had complained about some meat he had purchased. Asda staff had apparently sought to suggest over their internal email system that the officer's complaint was fraudulent.

In *Cubby* v *Compuserve*, a 1991 case, the complaint was that Compuserve provided an independently-monitored bulletin-board service dealing with journalism on which an unchecked and allegedly defamatory posting appeared. Compuserve maintained that it was an innocent distributor of the material and not a publisher and consequently could not be held responsible for matters appearing on the bulletin board that it did not actually know about or suspect.

The court considering the matter acknowledged the instantaneous nature of posting to the internet, accepted that it was simply not feasible for Compuserve to examine every posting and exonerated the company from liability.

The Compuserve case was, however, followed in 1995 by a case brought against online service provider Prodigy.

Prodigy was held liable for defamatory allegations of fraud made against a company called Stratton Oakmont on a Prodigy maintained bulletin board (*Stratton Oakmont, Inc.* v *Prodigy Services Co.*, 1995 WL 323710 (N.Y. Sup. Ct. 1995).

In the case against Prodigy, the plaintiffs alleged that defamatory statements had been posted by a third party on a bulletin board maintained on Prodigy. The plaintiffs sought to have Prodigy's liability tested by the standards applicable to publishers of information, as opposed to distributors. The significance of this differential was explained by the court: 'one who repeats or otherwise republishes a libel is subject to liability as if he had originally published it'.

In contrast, distributors such as book stores and libraries may be liable for defamatory statements of others only if they knew or had reason to know of the defamatory statement at issue. A distributor, or deliverer of defamatory material is considered a passive conduit and will not be found liable in the absence of fault.

The court concluded that Prodigy, based on the manner in which it had in the past conducted its business operations, was a publisher and not a distributor for defamation purposes. The court, in reaching this conclusion, relied on a number of factors, including:

- Public pronouncements by Prodigy that it was different from other services because it exercised efforts to control the content of what was published on its bulletin boards.
- Prodigy's promulgation of content guidelines.
- Prodigy's use of software screening programs to automatically pre-screen bulletin boards for certain offensive language; and
- Retention of board leaders to enforce the content guidelines with respect to particular bulletin boards. By attempting to exercise such editorial control over the content of its bulletin boards, (even though such attempts were by no means comprehensive or covering all messages posted to bulletin boards), the court held that Prodigy was subject to liability as a publisher, rather than a distributor.

The difference with the Compuserve case, the court held, was that Prodigy had specifically maintained that it regulated the contents of its bulletin boards so that it could market itself as a family oriented system. Consequently, Prodigy was held to be a publisher and not a mere innocent distributor of the defamatory material.

CHAPTER 11

Email and Internet Policies and Procedures

WHY HAVE A POLICY?

All employers should have a policy which makes it clear that excessive personal use of the internet and the accessing of pornography and other unsuitable material is strictly prohibited. By doing so, they will be in a far stronger position to take disciplinary action if an employee is caught misusing the resource in this way. An email and internet policy should tell employees whether, and to what extent, they may make use of the systems for personal use. In addition, types of websites and inappropriate email content should be defined. The consequences of breaching the policy should be made clear.

It is also important to incorporate such offences into both the disciplinary and equal opportunities policies. An employer may be vicariously liable for sexual harassment if an employee takes offence because other employees are accessing explicit images from the internet or because they are recipients of email with a sexual content to them.

In the case of *Morse* v *Future Reality* Case No: 54571/95 London North Employment Tribunal (see Chapters 4 and 5), an employee was successful in a sex discrimination claim, when her employer failed to take steps to prevent male colleagues from accessing pornography in the office which she shared with them.

By informing employees that behaviour of this sort will be considered a breach of the Equal Opportunities Policy an employer has a defence to a discrimination claim of this type. It is also extremely important that the procedure is implemented in practice. If employees are caught breaching the procedure, they should be disciplined. A failure to do this may prevent an employer from relying on the policy in the future.

Many employers will want to monitor the use of email and the internet. Any policy should warn employees of the use of monitoring software and the use of covert monitoring in light of the Human Rights Act 1998.

USE OF EMAIL

In less than a decade, email has asserted itself as the primary form of business communication, overtaking both the telephone and fax in terms of the number of calls made or faxes sent.

The growth of email has had a major economic effect. In the US alone, the postal service reported that mail traffic has fallen by five billion items annually compared with five years ago.

The popularity of email has created problems for businesses of all sizes.

STORING EMAIL

As well as being the most popular communications medium in business, email is also the biggest burden on IT storage. The explosion in use has led to colossal personal mailboxes and ever-increasing archiving and long-term storage needs.

One of the most frequently asked questions is how long do you need to store email? As with paper, there is a need to retain this information for a set period, but the exact time still remains vague.

The Data Protection Act 1998 says that data should be kept for as long as is necessary for the purpose it was obtained. The Chartered Institute for Personnel Development (CIPD) has produced a useful guide. For more information See their website: www.cipd.co.uk.

Organizations involved with financial services and litigation face particular problems in storing electronic data because there is no set time-frame during which it needs to be retained. Failure to store data for the required period can cause employers serious problems.

The Enron case highlighted what can happen when company data and documents are disposed of. In this case, Enron had grown from nowhere to be America's seventh largest company, employing 21 000 staff in more than 40 countries. The firm's success turned out to have involved an elaborate scam.

Enron had lied about its profits and stood accused of a range of shady dealings, including concealing debts so they didn't show up in the company's accounts.

As the depth of the deception unfolded, investors and creditors retreated, forcing the firm into Chapter 11 bankruptcy in December 2001.

On 15th June 2002, a jury in the United States found accountancy firm Arthur Andersen guilty of obstructing justice by shredding documents relating to the failed energy giant Enron. As a result, Andersen lost much of its business, and two-thirds of its once 28 000 strong US workforce. Following the conviction, there were multi-million dollar lawsuits brought by Enron investors and shareholders demanding compensation.

Enron's collapse in December 2001 was partly blamed on questionable accounting that kept hundreds of millions of dollars in debt off its books. Andersen, which audited Enron's accounts, went on trial in Houston, Texas, after allegations that employees had illegally destroyed thousands of documents and computer records relating to its scandal-hit client, which was based there.

Andersen also faced a fine of up to $500 000. The firm's lawyers had argued that the shredding of documents had been routine housekeeping, but the jury decided it was an attempt to thwart federal regulators investigating Enron. The trial heard how one Andersen executive said on a training video that if documents were shredded and then the investigators arrived, that would be good.

The prosecution's star witness was former Andersen partner David Duncan, who was in charge of the Enron audit team. He admitted obstructing justice in April and told jurors that he had signed an agreement with Andersen to present a united front, claiming that neither had done anything wrong. He said that he had reneged on the agreement after much 'soul searching'.

The verdict came after US District Court Judge Melinda Harmon made what is believed to be a landmark legal decision to break a deadlock among the jury. She ruled that jurors could reach a verdict on the company as a whole, even though they failed to agree on the individual responsible for ordering the shredding.

This is not just an example of a company disposing of information, it is more a case of inappropriate company guidelines. However, the process of archiving and managing stored data has been clarified by significant improvements in management software. Tools are now capable of mining stored email much more effectively, with many able to look inside exchange databases and extract single mails instantly from an archive.

HOW TO DRAW UP YOUR COMPANY EMAIL POLICY

A written policy sets out commonsense rules and fits them into a legal framework.

The following should be made clear:

- Employees have an email account because the company sees it as necessary for their work. It is a tool to assist with work.
- Just as with the telephone, the company may allow employees to use email for private correspondence. This is a privilege, not a right. Email should not be used for any other purposes than work and certain private reasons.
- While the company accepts that the employee has the right to privacy, the company reserves the right to check email if the company believes that an employee has been abusing email, such as using email for commercial purposes outside of the company's business; to access or pass on pornography or other unsuitable material; to harass or insult anyone.
- Employees should be aware that email has the same status in law as any other document and that insulting someone in an email may be considered defamatory and may leave the company and/or the individual employee open to legal action.

Other information should include:

- Spam is a menace and on no account should users click on links within spam messages. They should delete them.
- Viruses can harm systems. On no account should users activate attachments unless they are from a trusted source.

QUESTIONS AND ANSWERS

1) I am the head of IT. If my director asks me to provide him with access to someone's mailbox, where do I stand legally? Can I allow access?

The Codes of Practice published by the Information Commissioner have clarified this issue. The employee is entitled to privacy, which means that there is no absolute right to access an employee's email. However, you do have the right to allow access by a manager if there is a question of wrongdoing on the part of the employee.

If the manager wants access to the email because it contains something important and the employee is on holiday then you should seek the permission of the employee.

2) We are a magazine publishing company. How long do we need to retain data?

There are no special requirements for publishers other than those that apply in the case of libel. It is a good idea for journalists to keep all notes and supporting information relating to a story for at least three years, and the same rules can be applied to email.

3) We have a policy to delete all mail after six months. Is this acceptable as long as the policy is published?

No. If the policy is published you are covered for internal users, but the policy needs to work with the requirements for your particular company and the industry in which it works.

The UK parents of US subsidiaries are subject to US law and there are stringent requirements on how long you must keep email, post-Enron. A good rule is to keep everything but offload it onto low-cost storage. Good email management products and policies will help so that, for example, you do not store 500 copies of the same attachment.

4) What is the legal standpoint on staff storing emails on the C drive? How would this affect a customer asking for copies of all emails relating to them?

You should have all information stored centrally, but if information is only stored locally then it still will fall within the requirements of the DPA.

A number of company policies are set out in the Appendices.

APPENDICES

Policy Documents

POLICY 1

ELECTRONIC COMMUNICATIONS AT WORK POLICY

1. Introduction
2. Scope and Applicability
3. Objectives
4. Monitoring and Disciplinary Action
    - 4.1 Traffic Monitoring
    - 4.2 Content Monitoring
    - 4.3 Disciplinary Action
5. Internet and Email Acceptable Use Guidelines
    - 5.1 Background
    - 5.2 Court Service Implementation of Internet and Email Services
    - 5.3 Internet Services Authorised for Use
    - 5.4 General Guidelines
    - 5.5 Specific Guidelines for Internet Usage
    - 5.6 Specific Guidelines for Email Usage
    - 5.7 Personal use
    - 5.8 Summary
6. Mobile Phones
    - 6.1 Allocation of Mobile Phones
    - 6.2 Personal Use
    - 6.3 Short Messaging Service (SMS)
    - 6.4 Monitoring
    - 6.5 Paying for Personal Calls
    - 6.6 Security of Communications via Mobile Phones
    - 6.7 Health and Safety
    - 6.8 The Record of Mobile Phone Allocations
7. Landline Telephones
    - 7.1 Personal Use
    - 7.2 Security
8. Fax Machines
    - 8.1 Personal Use
    - 8.2 Transmission of Facsimiles
9. Remote Working
    - 9.1 Secure Remote Working
    - 9.2 Document Security
    - 9.3 Communications Security
10. Personal Digital Assistants (PDAs)
11. Video Conference Facilities

Annex 1 Legislation
- A.1.1 The Data Protection Act 1998
- A.1.2 European Convention on Human Rights
- A.1.4 Regulation of Investigatory Powers Act 2000
- A.1.5 The Telecommunications (Lawful Business Practice) (Interception of Communications) Regulations 2000
- A.1.6 The Freedom of Information Act 2000
- A.1.7 Obscene Publications Act 1959
- A.1.8 Telecommunications Act 1984
- A.1.9 Protection of Children Act 1978; Criminal Justice Act 1988
- A.1.10 Copyright, Design and Patents Act 1998
- A.1.11 Protection from Harassment Act 1997; Sex Discrimination Act 1975; Race Relations Act 1976
- A.1.12 Computer Misuse Act 1990

Annex 2 The Four Categories of Protective Marking: Definitions
- A.2.1 Top Secret
- A.2.2 Secret
- A.2.3 Confidential
- A.2.4 Restricted

Annex 3 Glossary

1. Introduction

Dear Colleague

Today, email, the internet, fax machines, voicemail and video conferencing are commonplace in most government offices. They have brought about fast and efficient means of communication that are increasingly accepted as standard business practice.

In March 1999 the Cabinet Office published Electronic Communications at Work: what you need to know. This recommended that departments and agencies should have a policy statement or code of practice on electronic communications.

This policy is relevant to all users of IT systems and electronic communication devices issued by the Court Service. It is particularly relevant to senior managers with responsibility for policy on the use and monitoring of electronic communications and for line managers concerned with the procedures that need to be followed if abuse is suspected.

In this policy and guidance we wish to encourage, in particular, greater use of email and the internet to help users perform their work. We also want to highlight important management and legal issues that need to be considered before access is granted.

Our aim is to ensure a consistent policy on electronic communications throughout the Court Service. Therefore in consultation with Trade Union Side and staff representatives, this comprehensive policy is being introduced.

Users accessing or otherwise using Court Service Electronic Communications facilities, whether for the conduct of official business, or for personal use must read this document and acknowledge that they have received the document. Users of electronic communications facilities must adhere to the guidelines articulated in this document and all other Court Service policies relating to personal conduct.

It is the responsibility of line managers to support implementation of Court Service policies. It is also the responsibility of users to seek clarification of any aspect of these policies from their line manager.

Yours sincerely

Mr X
Head of Corporate Services

2. Scope and Applicability

This overarching policy document is comprised of guidance on the use of the following:

- internet
- email
- mobile phones
- telephones
- faxes
- secure remote working
- personal digital assistants
- video conferencing

The policy applies to all users and users or agents of other organizations/ departments (internal or external to the Court Service) who use, directly or indirectly support or interface with the department's IS/IT services and communication systems and devices.

3. Objectives

The Electronic Communications At Work Policy has the following objectives:

- To ensure security measures are practicable, risk based and cost effective.
- To ensure the Court Service complies with legal requirements and other obligations.
- To maintain confidentiality – to prevent unauthorised disclosure of information.
- To maintain the integrity of information and other assets – to prevent modification of information or other assets through unintended or malicious changes, and
- To maintain the availability of employee's information and other assets.

These aims will be achieved by the designation of responsibilities and the departmental arrangements specified in the following sections.

It is recognised the effectiveness of this Policy requires the cooperation of all users.

4. Monitoring and Disciplinary Action

4.1 Traffic Monitoring

Users should note that the Court Service routinely monitors the use of IT and all communication facilities. This is to ensure compliance with security and other regulations, and to ensure operational effectiveness, as is permitted by legislation. It follows from this that users of Electronic Communication facilities, should be aware, and must accept as a condition of use, that their business and personal usage of such facilities is monitored.

Use is routinely monitored, and may be specifically monitored at any time when this is deemed necessary for compliance or other reasons, including the prevention or detection of illegal activities.

Users should not, therefore, have any expectation of privacy in relation to their use of communication facilities whether that use is for business or permitted personal purposes.

Normal monitoring will take the form of traffic monitoring. Through the normal monitoring process, traffic monitoring may be targeted at business areas or individuals where abuse is suspected.

The Information Security Officer (ISO – Adam Stranger on TELEPHONE NUMBER) is responsible for the analysis of all usage reports.

4.2 Content Monitoring

Analysis of traffic reports may highlight areas of concern and abuse of the communication facilities. Where there is a suspected case of abuse the ISO will prepare a preliminary report to the Head of HRU and the relevant Business Manager. Where the suspected case of abuse is a Level 1 or above the ISO will prepare a preliminary report to the Director of Corporate Services or to the Director as appropriate.

For further examination into the content of the information, authority for investigation must be sought from the Head of HRU. Only upon this authority can the ISO instigate the gathering of this information.

The ISO will be able to gather the following information:

- All internet pages that were visited including any images that were viewed.
- All emails sent and received.
- Records of telephone calls made and received, including the number (internal and external) and the duration of the calls made.
- Records of mobile phone calls made and received, including the number and the duration of the calls made.
- Records of fax messages sent and received.
- This information may be used for the conduction of a disciplinary procedure.

4.3 Disciplinary Action

All Court Service policies pertaining to personal conduct apply when using any of the electronic facilities as outlined in paragraph 2 particularly those that deal with intellectual property protection, privacy, misuse of Court Service resources, information and data security (including confidentiality), sexual harassment and other discriminatory practices.

Where a Business Manager suspects a breach of the Electronic Communications at Work Policy they must contact the Head of HRU. The Head of HRU will formally instruct the ISO to conduct an investigation. The ISO will advise whether a breach has occurred and the relevant part/s of the policy.

Disciplinary action will be in accordance with the Northern Ireland Court Service Discipline procedures. All users must be aware that inappropriate use of Court Service electronic facilities may result in disciplinary action, which may, in some cases, result in dismissal.

Users should also be aware that the findings of the investigation may lead to criminal proceedings in certain instances.

5. Internet and Email Acceptable Use Guidelines

5.1 Background

The Court Service is very aware of the benefits and advantages that use of the internet and email can deliver and are equally aware of the potential dangers that careless or negligent use may incur. For example, unnecessary, unauthorised internet and email usage may cause network and server congestion, slow service delivery, reduce efficiency, consume supplies, and tie up shared resources. Furthermore, unlawful or careless usage may result in negative publicity for the Court Service and could lead to potential legal liabilities. Users should note that they could be personally liable to prosecution, and open to claims for damages from aggrieved individuals, if their actions are found to be in breach of the law.

In designing mechanisms to ensure that users are aware of this internet and email policy, the Court Service has taken account of the requirements of the Lawful Business Practice Regulations 2000, which require employers to inform users, that communication interceptions, even of private communications, might take place.

Users must, at all times, conduct themselves honestly and appropriately when accessing the internet and email facilities.

This includes:

- respecting copyrights
- software licensing rules
- property rights
- the privacy and legitimate rights of others.

Users must be aware that inappropriate use of Court Service internet and email facilities may result in disciplinary action, which may, in some cases, include dismissal.

All Court Service policies pertaining to personal conduct apply when using the internet and email, particularly those that deal with intellectual property protection, privacy, misuse of Court Service resources, information and data security (including confidentiality), sexual harassment and other discriminatory practices.

5.2 Court Service Implementation of Internet and Email Services

All offices in the Court Service are linked to Fujitsu's Trident House using an accredited internal network with appropriate firewall protection, which protects the Court Service internal network from all other networks. The Court Service provides a connection to the internet by way of a high-speed link. This provides the link from the internal Court Service network onto the external internet network to allow users to access internet services from their PC.

The Government Secure Internet (GSI) is a system that connects UK government departments from, in our case, the Court Service network. The GSI links departments whose internal networks are accredited to a protective marking of Restricted.

The Court Service has developed an intranet website. This is a website which resides within the Court Service network and has a protective marking of Restricted. The intranet site provides information of particular relevance to Court Service users and other users of IT services. The intranet website also provides links to websites on the internet. This can be used as a convenient link onto the internet.

The connection via the Court Service network allows Court Service users to have an email address from which they can send and receive email between other government departments who are connected to the GSI.

All users have access to internal and external email facilities. External email accounts are allocated on a business need as determined by the Programme Executive.

5.3 Internet Services Authorised for Use

Internet services, which are authorised and available for use, are as follows:

- access to the Court Service intranet website;
- access to the Court Service internet website;
- universal access to the World Wide Web (internet);
- universal access to GSI services.

5.4 General Guidelines

The Court Service wishes to encourage employees' usage of the internet, as the internet is a source of valuable business information. The Court Service also wishes to encourage employees' usage of email facilities. Email can speed up correspondence dramatically.

User IDs and passwords help maintain individual accountability for internet and email services usage, and protection for individuals against fraud and misuse. Any member of staff who obtains a password or ID for an internet resource must keep that password confidential in accordance with the Court Service Departmental IT Security Policy.

Any file that is downloaded from the internet to the Court Service network will be scanned for viruses before access to the file is granted.

Users are not permitted to download any executable file (see glossary p. 179) from the internet.

The Court Service uses internet firewalls to assure the safety and security of its internal network. Any user who attempts to disable, defeat or circumvent these will be subject to appropriate disciplinary action.

Most of the information used or transmitted by the Court Service will attract a protective marking of Restricted. This means that you may only allow the information to be transferred internally on the Court Service network or through the GSI to other government departments. Protectively-marked information cannot be transmitted over the internet.

Users must respect the privacy and the legitimate rights of others, just as would be appropriate in any other work activity. Users must, at all times, conduct themselves honestly and appropriately when using internet and email facilities.

Users must not:

- place at risk the integrity, security or operation of Court Service IT systems or equipment;
- engage in any action or activity, which would place themselves as individuals or the Court Service, liable to criminal prosecution or civil action;

- create any unauthorised contractual liability on the part of the Court Service;
- access or disseminate any inappropriate material;
- create, access or disseminate any offensive material, including but not limited to, material of a sectarian, racial, sexually explicit, discriminatory or defamatory nature;
- engage in any action, which would bring the Court Service into disrepute.

Users must report immediately:

- any indication of a virus or other attack;
- any inadvertent accessing of inappropriate or offensive material;
- receipt of unsolicited inappropriate or offensive material.

Users must be aware that inappropriate use of internet facilities may result in disciplinary action, which may, in some cases, include dismissal.

All policies pertaining to personal conduct apply when using the internet and email, particularly those that deal with intellectual property protection, privacy, misuse of departmental/ agency resources, information and data security (including confidentiality), sexual harassment and other discriminatory practices.

5.5 Specific Guidelines for Internet Usage

Access to certain types of websites has been restricted. Currently the areas of restriction are as follows:

- adult entertainment
- gambling
- hacking
- illegal activities
- militancy
- racism
- sex

- tasteless/ offensive
- violence
- weapons
- web chat.

Users must not participate in chat rooms, discussion forums or newsgroups unless this is for business purposes and has been approved by the Business Manager, in consultation with the Information Security Officer.

Users must not download or install any internet application, Internet Explorer browser enhancement or plug in.

Users must not play online games at any time.

5.6 Specific Guidelines for Email Usage

Users must not:

- place at risk the integrity, security or operation of Court Service IT systems or equipment;
- carry out any action or activity which would place themselves as individuals or the Court Service, liable to criminal prosecution or civil action;
- creating any unauthorised contractual liability on the part of the Court Service;
- access or disseminate any inappropriate material;
- creating, accessing or disseminating any offensive material, including but not limited to, material of a sectarian, racial, sexually explicit, discriminatory or defamatory nature;
- take any action, which would bring the Court Service into disrepute.

Users must report immediately receipt of unsolicited inappropriate or offensive material to the ISO.

Users must be aware that inappropriate use of email facilities may result in disciplinary action, which may, in some cases, include dismissal.

All personal emails, whether internal or external, must be clearly marked as being 'personal'. The subject line must be marked 'PERSONAL'. Users must also include a disclaimer statement at the start of the email, which says:

> *This email represents personal views of the sender and is not sent on behalf of the Northern Ireland Court Service.*

There may well be personal emails relating to your employment or terms and conditions, for example, sensitive communications between HRU and you. Such emails should be marked 'PERSONAL BUSINESS'.

The use of Web Mail, such as Hotmail, is prohibited. As individuals are permitted personal use of the email system there is no requirement for users to use this facility.

Sending Court Service documents across a Web Mail facility is prohibited.

Users should note that business managers could, in conjunction with a HRU representative, for legitimate business processing purposes, check the mailboxes of absent users. While it is not intended to undertake routine monitoring of the content of emails (personal or otherwise) content may be accessed at any time either as a result of checking an officer's email account for business reasons if they are absent from work, or as part of an exercise to monitor compliance with internet and email usage policy.

In the normal course of events, emails marked 'PERSONAL' or 'PERSONAL BUSINESS' will not be read except where a crime or commissioning of a crime is being investigated. However, in certain circumstances, for example, where an officer is absent and may be for some time, it may be necessary for emails marked 'PERSONAL BUSINESS' to be opened and read by suitably authorised users for processing. Only the Head of HRU can give the authority for this action to be taken and they must assure themselves that there is justification for doing so.

It is an explicit condition of using the email facility that users accept that the content of emails may be accessed by the appropriate management and/or security users in accordance with the above statements without any further notice or any requirement for consent.

The Court Service will automatically place at the end of all external emails the following disclaimer:

This email (and any attachment) is intended only for the attention of the addressee(s). Its unauthorised use, disclosure, storage or copying is not permitted. If you are not the intended recipient, please destroy all copies and inform the sender by return email.

Internet email is not a secure medium. Any reply to this message could be intercepted and read by someone else. Please bear that in mind when deciding whether to send material in response to this message by email.

This email (whether you are the sender or the recipient) may be monitored, recorded and retained by the Northern Ireland Court Service. Email monitoring and blocking software may be used, and email content may be read at any time. You have a responsibility to ensure laws are not broken when composing or forwarding emails and their contents.

With this in mind, and in the full knowledge that the Court Service monitors all emails, users can choose whether or not to make permitted personal use of the email system.

Users must not promote or participate in chain mail. Chain mail has the potential to overload the email system and to cause distress or offence to those who receive it.

To enable compliance with a wide range of statutory duties and responsibilities, the Court Service has a duty to keep a permanent record of all significant documents. At present, this means that a paper copy of any important or significant email must be made and filed. While judgment is needed about what is significant or important, a paper copy is needed where the email message contains material which:

- provides the only evidence of the origin of and/or date of receipt of an attached document which needs to be retained;
- records decisions or provides authority for action;
- will be needed to maintain business continuity;
- might be needed for administrative, accounting, audit, research or historical purposes;
- might be needed to prove whether an activity or transaction took place; and/or

- could be requested under the Data Protection or Freedom of Information provisions.

As is the case with external or internal mail being sent to the wrong person, it is the responsibility of the officer who receives the mail to ensure that email is properly re-directed or returned to the originator.

5.7 Personal Use

Personal use is defined as any use of Electronic Communication facilities, which does not stem from a requirement directly relating to the officers official duties. Thus accessing news or other sites for data relevant to an area of work – for example, researching social security, or employment law developments – is official use if, and only if, such access is necessary as a direct part of the officer's work. If an officer chooses to access such data out of personal interest, or to broaden his or her knowledge of government policy in that area, but does not actually require the information in order to discharge their duties effectively, the access should be classed as personal use.

Personal use of email is defined as any use of internal or external email facilities, which does not stem from a requirement directly relating to the officers official duties.

Users should note that permission for personal use is not a right, it is a facility which may be given at the discretion of management and it may be withdrawn at any time for operational reasons, or if abuse is suspected or detected.

Users may use internet facilities for personal research, and so on,, provided such use takes place in their own time, has been approved by local management, and complies with this Usage Policy and other relevant departmental policies.

Users may make occasional use of email accounts set up on their behalf, to send, forward or receive personal emails, subject to the conditions for using email facilities set out in this policy.

Users may, in their own time; use the internet for the occasional purchase of goods and services (for example, books, flights, CDs), provided payment is made by the individual, and delivery of items purchased is to a private address. Users may also, in their own time, make occasional use of internet facilities for 'online banking'. Note that all such use is at the risk of the individual; the Court

Service will not accept liability for losses or other liabilities to the individual arising out of any such transactions.

5.8 Summary

- Access to certain categories of websites is restricted.
- Users must not participate in chat rooms, discussion forums or newsgroups without authorisation.
- Users must not download any software, application or plug in.
- Online games may not be played at any time.
- Personal use of the internet is subject to local business manager discretion.
- Personal use of the internet must take place in user's own time.
- Personal use of email facilities is subject to local business manager discretion.
- All 'personal' or 'personal business' emails must be marked so in the subject line and include a disclaimer.
- Court Service users will not open 'personal' or 'personal business' emails without justification and proper authorisation.
- Users must not participate in chain mails.
- Users must print out emails if they form part of official records.

6. Mobile Phones

The purpose of these guidelines is to draw your attention to those matters, which must be taken into consideration before, and while using departmental mobile phones. The content defines the Court Service policy for all users based on guidance contained within the Manual of Protective Security published by the Cabinet Office.

The Inland Revenue publication entitled 'Expenses and Benefits – a Tax Guide 480 (1997)' defines a mobile phone as:

> *A phone not physically connected to a landline and includes a car phone, even when the car is taxable as a company car. It does not include a cordless phone (that is, a phone used only as an extension to another*

phone which is physically connected to a landline), or a telephonist phone (equipment providing a short-range phone service within a specified waveband and which can only be used within a few metres of a fixed point).

The Court Service aims to encourage reasonable, responsible and well-informed behaviour coupled with good management practice. All members of the Court Service need to be aware of this policy, both as individuals and, where applicable as managers, since the use of mobile telecommunications raises significant management and legal issues. Used properly, a mobile phone will help you to do your job more effectively and help the Court Service improve its business performance and achieve its objectives. If you are unclear as to how you are affected, please consult your line manager.

Mobile phone users are required to take due care of the equipment and safeguard it from loss and damage. In the event of loss and damage anyone not able to prove due care may be liable for the cost of replacing the equipment. As such, it is advisable that users allocated a mobile phone should ensure they are insured against any such loss.

The number of mobile phone thefts has greatly increased and consideration should be given to when and where calls are made or taken. Many phones are also stolen from unattended cars. On receipt of a mobile phone users must use the phone's security lock code. If you are unsure how to enable this facility please contact Procurement Branch. The following information will also help to keep your mobile phone safe:

- keep your phone out of sight in your pocket or handbag when not in use;
- use your phone's security lock code (PIN);
- property mark your phone with your postcode and door number to help police identify stolen ones;
- report a lost or stolen phone to the Procurement Branch immediately.

As a general guide users should not:

- attract attention to your phone when you are carrying or using it in the street;
- park in isolated or dark areas;

- Leave your phone in an unattended car. If you must, lock it out of sight.

6.1 Allocation of Mobile Phones

The criteria for allocation of mobile phones are as follows:

- Level 1 users and above.
- Peripatetic users where the individuals absence from their headquarters exceeds 50 per cent of normal working hours and there is a clear business requirement.
- Users covering on call or call out arrangements (allocation may be on a pool basis).
- Business need supported by a written case authorised by the Business Manager.

In the event that a user no longer satisfies the above criteria the Business Manager should inform Procurement Branch and either return the handset or re-allocate to a qualifying user.

6.2 Personal Use

A mobile phone is a taxable benefit unless there are either no personal calls or an employee pays for all personal calls. Therefore, if you use an official mobile phone to make a personal call you must declare and pay for it. Failure to declare a personal call is a breach of both Inland Revenue and Court Service rules. Disciplinary action will be taken where there is a deliberate attempt to defraud the Department. Personal use, as defined by the Inland Revenue is:

> *Calls that are not wholly, exclusively and necessarily in the performance of the employee's duties, and includes private reverse charge calls.*

It is important to note that in the event of a breakdown during business travel, emergency calls made from the mobile phone are not classed as 'private use'. However, such calls made during private travel (including home to office travel) are regarded as private use and the user must repay the cost of the call.

6.3 Short Messaging Service (SMS)

The use of the Short Message Service (SMS) is restricted to purely business use. Users should take into account the content of such messages as

SMS messages are subject to all the applicable laws such as those relating to copyright, defamation, data protection, public records, discrimination and harassment. Users are reminded that transmitting material of this type is an abuse of facilities and is considered unacceptable behaviour.

Users must not subscribe to SMS or text alert services offered by various service providers.

Members of the Court Service should not respond to any unsolicited SMS or text messages.

6.4 Monitoring

All mobile phone bills received by the Court Service include itemised call charges. Mobile phone users are required to have sight of the breakdown of calls made from their mobile every month to identify and highlight all personal calls made, as set out in RIB Awareness Alerter <http://ncttrint2/nictsweb/Courts/RMB.htm>. Individuals are trusted to declare and pay for personal calls. Line managers should also have sight of itemised bills, as it is their responsibility to satisfy themselves that the mobile phone user has identified all personal calls and to query with the user any calls that appear to be private. The Department provides mobile phones for business purposes, and as such, private calls should only be a very small percentage of the total calls shown on an invoice. It is the responsibility of the line manager to monitor and evaluate the business benefits of mobile phone use within their remit. It is recommended that personal calls should not exceed, on average, more than 25 per cent of the total number of calls made.

6.5 Paying For Personal Calls

The Department does recognise that users may need to make occasional private calls but the full cost of the call must be reimbursed to the Department. In accordance with the RMB Awareness Alerter and the desk notes issued simultaneously regarding the recoupment of personal calls, the user should pay for all personal calls by forwarding a cheque, made payable to 'HM Paymaster General' for the correct amount, to their local payments team. This will be forwarded to RMB.

Any loyalty bonus granted on an invoice belongs to the Department and should not therefore be deducted in whole or in part from the costs of any private use for example, a bundle of 'free' airtime such as 20 minutes of free calls. The terms of the government contract under which the Court Service mobile phones operates already includes an agreed corporate discount rate which is the only loyalty bonus which should be awarded. If you have any queries regarding how this may affect you please contact Procurement Branch for advice.

6.6 Security of Communications via Mobile Phones

There are no limitations within the UK on the use of digital mobile phones for 'Restricted' information. Digital mobile phones should not be used outside the UK for 'protectively marked' communications. Annex 1 attached will provide further information on the distinctions within security markings.

6.7 Health and Safety

In 1999 the Government commissioned the National Radiological Protection Board (NRPB) to set up an Independent Expert Group on Mobile Phones (IEGMP) who would investigate the health risks from the use of mobile phones. The IEGMP published a report in May 2000, which concluded that mobile phones do comply with NRPB guideline levels on exposure to non-ionising electromagnetic radiation. They advised however that a 'precautionary approach should be adopted until more robust scientific information becomes available'.

An information leaflet has been published on the advice of the IEGMP entitled 'Mobile phones and health' the content of which can be found on the Department of Health (GB) website <http://www.doh.gov.uk/mobile.htm>. The Court Service would encourage a user that has concerns about using the mobile phone allocated to them to avail of this service and to contact Procurement Branch if they wish to discuss their concerns.

This Department also supports the view of the IEGMP that 'the use of mobile phones whilst driving can substantially increase the risk of an accident and that drivers should be dissuaded from using either hand-held or hands-free phones whilst on the move'.

Users should therefore not attempt to use a mobile phone whilst driving and should note that to drive a car without proper control is an offence under the Road Traffic NI Order 1981 and that an offender can be prosecuted. For your safety and that of other road users, use voicemail or divert calls so that messages can be left while your phone is switched off.

Separate guidance on safe driving and the use of mobile phones has been published by the Department for Transport, Environment and the Regions (DETR) in their leaflet 'Mobile Phones and Driving'. Copies of this leaflet are available in Procurement Branch upon request. Existing and future members of users allocated a mobile phone for business purposes shall receive a copy of this literature. If you do not receive your copy, contact Procurement Branch immediately.

6.8 The Record of Mobile Phone Allocations

Procurement Branch maintains a record of every mobile phone allocated to users for audit and asset management purposes. Users should not enter into independent negotiations with the mobile phone services provider for additional equipment without prior agreement with Procurement Branch. Mobile phone accessories are provided with each new phone. If additional or replacement accessories are required they should be ordered through Procurement Branch.

All policies pertaining to personal conduct apply when using mobile phones, particularly those that deal with intellectual property protection, privacy, misuse of departmental/ agency resources, information and data security (including confidentiality), sexual harassment and other discriminatory practices.

7. Landline Telephones

7.1 Personal Use

Occasional and reasonable use of official landline telephones (not mobile phones) is permitted without charge. Line managers should satisfy themselves that personal use of an official landline telephone is not excessive and is within reason. Users should be aware that a desktop telephone is the most cost-effective way of making a telephone call.

7.2 Security

There are no limitations within the UK on the use of the normal public telephone network for Restricted information.

No protectively-marked communication should be made using an analogue mobile telephone, a cordless phone, or where there is a manual switchboard.

Communications protectively-marked Confidential and above within the UK, and communications protectively-marked Restricted outside the UK, should be protected by using secure official telephones.

If there is a need to conduct conversations that are protectively-marked Confidential_please contact the Departmental Security Officer in Procurement Branch who will arrange for the use of a secure telephone line.

All policies pertaining to personal conduct apply when using landline telephones, particularly those that deal with intellectual property protection, privacy, misuse of departmental/ agency resources, information and data security (including confidentiality), sexual harassment and other discriminatory practices.

8. Fax Machines

8.1 Personal Use

Occasional and reasonable use of official fax machines is permitted without charge.

The distribution or causing to be distributed material which is considered undesirable, such as pornography or political extremism, is an abuse of facilities, is considered unacceptable behaviour and may be subject to disciplinary action and/or legal proceedings. Users should be aware that each fax sent from a departmental fax facility will declare full transmission details to the recipient. This will identify the date, day and time of the transmission plus the Department from which the fax was broadcast, that is, the Court Service and the fax number.

All policies pertaining to personal conduct apply when using fax facilities, particularly those that deal with intellectual property protection, privacy, misuse of departmental/agency resources, information and data security (including confidentiality), sexual harassment and other discriminatory practices.

8.2 Transmission of Facsimiles

A standard fax machine may be used to transmit documents protectively-marked Restricted. However, before sending them, you must verify the recipient's fax number and they must be on standby at their machine to collect the copies. Only a secure fax facility within the Department's premises may be used for documents marked Confidential and above.

9. Remote Working

9.1 Secure Remote Working

Although remote working is widely associated with home working, this policy also applies equally to other types of remote working, for example, in hotel rooms and at conference venues. Since other locations inevitably are less secure than official premises, you should avoid taking protectively-marked material away from your office. However, there are occasions when you may find it necessary to undertake work at a remote location. In those circumstances you have a special responsibility to ensure that the public interest justifies the risk of removing any documents from the office, especially those, which are protectively marked. You must appreciate the need for safe custody of official papers or equipment once they have been taken away from the normal business premises and you should not 'advertise' the fact that you work on official information remotely, especially if that involves working at home.

If you are a Line Manager, you should not allow protectively-marked material to be taken out of the office unless you are satisfied that the users concerned understand their obligations to protect such material. All necessary practical arrangements must have been made to ensure physical security measures are in place.

The guidance applies only in the UK. Where individuals are required to work on such assets overseas, specific security guidance will be needed due to the differing levels of threat posed by the country or countries involved.

This section applies equally to paper or electronic documents.

When dealing with official documents at home or elsewhere outside the office you should, as far as possible, adhere to the following guidelines.

- Personal and official matters should be kept physically apart and protectively-marked material must always be stored in the appropriate secure containers.
- You must have a designated working area, preferably in a lockable room. If that is not possible you should work in an area where any interruptions can be controlled or kept to a minimum. Additionally,

the equivalent of a clear desk policy should be applied when you are not occupying the room or area.

- If you are interrupted you should ensure that visitors or members of your household do not overlook official papers.
- Log off IT equipment when it is unattended.

9.2 Document Security

This section applies equally to paper or electronic documents.

Authority/approval

You must obtain appropriate written authority to remove protectively-marked documents from the office as follows:

Top Secret	Personal authority of Director
Secret	Authority of Head of Division or above
Confidential	Authority of a Business Manager or above
Restricted	Authority of your line manager

Registration

If you have to undertake any form of remote working you and your line manager must maintain an information register of protectively-marked assets removed from official premises. You should also use the register to record any protectively-marked documents, discs, tapes, and so on, that you create while working remotely. Entries should be comprehensive showing addressees to whom assets have been dispatched, the asset's destruction (if appropriate) or a file reference where a document has been filed.

Transportation

Documents taken out of the office must be kept in a locked briefcase or box, secured official laptop or pc, or other appropriate container and remain with you on any journey between locations.

Storage

At home, or any other locations away from the office, protectively-marked material and its container must remain at all times in your immediate possession unless you have access to a proper security container approved for the level of protection required. If you take protectively-marked material home on a regular basis you should be provided with an appropriate security container or secured portable pc. If your home is unoccupied for longer than five days all protectively-marked material must be returned to the office.

Photocopying

The photocopying of documents protectively-marked Confidential or higher is only permitted using official equipment within departmental premises. When making copies of Restricted papers using local commercial facilities you should undertake the copying and should refrain from using digital photocopiers since they retain an image of copied documents. You must ensure that documents are not read or identified as official material by other individuals.

Waste

All protectively-marked or sensitive waste material must be returned to the office for destruction. Disks and laptops or PCs holding protectively marked data must be disposed of securely. For the latest advice you should contact the Information Security Officer.

9.3 Communications Security

Telephones

There are no limitations within the UK on the use of the normal public telephone network or digital mobile phones for Restricted information. However, no protectively-marked communication should be made using an analogue mobile telephone, a cordless phone, or where there is a manual switchboard. Communications protectively-marked Confidential and above within the UK, and communications protectively-marked Restricted outside the UK, should be protected by using secure official telephones. Digital mobile telephones should not be used outside the UK for protectively-marked communications.

IT Security

The measures specified previously for room and document security apply equally in the case of anyone using either a desktop PC or a portable PC away from their office. Electronic documents are susceptible to the same risks as manual ones, with the following additions:

- The equipment holding the data is attractive to thieves.
- The volume of data that can be readily accessed is much greater (the contents of many filing cabinets can be held on a single hard disk).
- The data may be recoverable even after the owner thinks it has been erased.
- There is the possibility that a virus may be introduced that will compromise the integrity or availability of the data.
- If communication links are used, for example, internet, there is the risk of hacking or interception of the data in transit.

As a result of these additional risks the following policy has been adopted

You may only process protectively-marked material on equipment provided by the Court Service. Non-protectively-marked material may be processed on equipment not issued by the Court Service. To enable work to continue on an existing non-protectively-marked document in electronic form, you may either mail it to your home pc or download it on to a floppy disk.

Outside the office environment electronic processing of protectively marked data is permitted only on portable or desktop pcs supplied by the Court Service and provided the appropriate access controls and approved encryption have been installed. Portables and desktop pcs holding data protectively marked Confidential or above must not have an internet connection. The remote processing of confidential material must be carried out offline in the encrypted folder. Portables and desktop pcs holding Restricted data may have email connections provided the appropriate access controls and encryption software is installed and any Restricted email must be encrypted before it is transmitted through the Internet.

The guidance set out in the IT Security Policy regarding the security of portable pcs must be applied at all times.

Any officer accessing any IT services remotely on Court Service equipment must be aware of the IT Security Policy and the other guideline documents set out in the Electronic Communications at Work Policy.

If you have any queries about working with IT equipment at remote locations you should contact the Information Security Officer.

10. Personal Digital Assistants (PDAs)

Only officially issued PDAs may be used to store protectively marked information up to Restricted level.

Users must physically protect the PDA the prevent opportunist theft and accidental damage.

If a PDA is lost or lost and recovered, this must be reported to the ISO.

Users must not use any infrared wireless or radio link functionality to communicate with other devices.

11. Video Conference Facilities

Video Conferencing facilities are only suitable for the conduct of information exchanges that are protectively-marked Restricted. The facility is not suitable for the exchange of information at protectively-marked Confidential or higher.

Annex 1 Legislation

A.1.1 The Data Protection Act 1998

The Data Protection Act 1998 (DPA) requires departments and agencies to process personal data 'fairly' and 'lawfully'.

Personal data means information about identifiable living individuals and includes both facts and opinions about the individual. The DPA provides for individuals to be provided with a copy, on request, of the personal data an organization holds on them. This includes personal data collected by any monitoring. You must have polices and procedures in place to deal with any requests if they are made.

The DPA does not just apply to data held on large databases. Any set of data held electronically, including material held on a personal computer, is potentially disclosable. This includes any references to an individual in any document, file, folder or email, including emails still in the 'deleted' folder. Although there has been a tendency to consider emails as an informal or fleeting way of communicating, the data they contain is subject to the same disclosure provisions as data elsewhere. Directories containing names, telephone numbers, email addresses, and so on, also fall within the scope of the Act. The DPA also applies to certain collections of non-computerised personal information, such as printouts of emails held in structured filing systems. It is crucial to ensure that anything created is accurate, relevant and justifiable, and that data and emails no longer necessary for business are fully deleted.

The Information Commissioner's forthcoming Code of Practice on the Use of Personal Data in Employer/Employee Relationships will set data protection standards in this area.

You will be able to obtain further information from the Departmental Data Protection Officer, who is based in the Information Centre, Ground Floor, Windsor House, Belfast. Further information can also be found on the Information Commissioners site at <http://www.dataprotection.gov.uk/>.

A.1.2 European Convention on Human Rights

A public sector employee invoked the European Convention on Human Rights after her employer intercepted her telephone calls (*Halford* v *UK Government*). The European Court of Human Rights found that the secret interception of calls made by Ms Halford from her office amounted to an unjustifiable interference with her right to respect for her privacy and correspondence, contrary to Article 8(1) of the European Convention on Human Rights.

A.1.3 Human Rights Act 1998

The Human Rights Act 1998 incorporated the European Convention on Human Rights into domestic law. Under this Act a UK citizen is be able to assert their Convention rights through the national courts without having to take their case to the European Court of Human Rights.

Further information on the Human Rights Act can be found on the Home Office site <http://www.homeoffice.gov.uk/hract/hramenu.htm>.

A.1.4 Regulation of Investigatory Powers Act 2000

Part I of the Regulation of Investigatory Powers Act 2000 (RIPA) makes it unlawful for employers and others to intercept communications, in the course of their transmission on a private telecommunications system, unless certain conditions are met. Interception is allowed where:

- the parties to the call, email or other communication have both consented to the interception, or
- the interception is of communications taking place using the employer's business telecommunications system and is authorised under The Telecommunications (Lawful Business Practice) (Interception of Communications) Regulations 2000.

RIPA only restricts access to the contents of a communication. It does not address the collection and use of traffic data on a private network, for example, the information about telephone calls that would typically be produced by a call logger. This is subject only to the requirements of the Data Protection Act 1998.

Further information on RIPA can be found on the Home Office site <http://www.homeoffice.gov.uk/ripa/ripact.htm>.

A.1.5 The Telecommunications (Lawful Business Practice)(Interception of Communications) Regulations 2000

The Lawful Business Practice Regulations authorize certain interceptions of communications that would otherwise be prohibited under RIPA 2000. The interception has to be by or with the consent of a person carrying on a business (which includes the activities of government departments, public authorities and others exercising statutory functions), for purposes relevant to that person's business, and using that business's own telecommunication system.

The Regulations authorize monitoring or recording without consent for the following purposes:

- to establish the existence of facts relevant to the business;
- to ascertain compliance with regulatory or self-regulatory practices or procedures relevant to the business;
- to ascertain or demonstrate standards which are achieved or ought to be achieved by those using the system;
- to prevent or detect crime;
- to investigate or detect unauthorised use of the business telecommunication systems.
- to ensure the effective operation of the system.

The Regulations also authorise businesses to monitor, but not record, communications transmitted over their systems without the employee's consent for the following purposes:

- check whether communications are relevant to the business;
- monitor calls to confidential counselling or support helplines run free of charge.

Interceptions are authorised only if the controller of the telecommunications system on which they are affected has made all reasonable efforts to inform potential users that interceptions may be made. The Regulations do not authorize interceptions to which the persons making and receiving the communications have consented: they are not prohibited by the Act.

Further information on the Regulations can be found on the Department of Trade and Industry (DTI) website <http://www.dti.gov.uk/cii/regulatory/telecomms/telecommsregulations/lawful_business_practice_regulations.shtml>.

The Regulations are available on the Her Majesty's Stationery Office (HMSO) website at: http://www.opsi.gov.uk/si/si2000/20002699.htm.

A.1.6 The Freedom of Information Act 2000

The Freedom of Information Act (FOIA) gives a general right of access to information held by departments. In due course it will replace the existing code of practice on Access to Government Information. The Act also amends certain provisions of the Public Records and Data Protection Acts. It provides clear statutory rights for those requesting information together with a strong enforcement regime. Under the terms of the Act, any member of the public will be able to apply for access to recorded information held by bodies across the public sector.

The legislation will apply to a wide range of public authorities, including Parliament, government departments and local authorities, health trusts, doctors' surgeries, publicly funded museums and thousands of other organizations.

The Act gives a general right of access to information held by public authorities in the course of carrying out their public functions, subject to certain conditions and exemptions.

Together these Statutes place a duty on departments and agencies to manage records, including emails, in such a way that their provisions can be complied with.

You should be able to obtain further information from those in your department dealing with the FOIA. Further information can also be found on the Information Commissioner's website <www.informationcommissioner.gov.uk>.

A.1.7 Obscene Publications Act 1959

All computer material is subject to this Act, under which it is a criminal offence to publish an article whose effect, taken as a whole, would tend to deprave and corrupt those likely to read, see or hear it.

A computer disk, including the principal hard disk of the computer, can constitute an obscene article for the purposes of this Act if it contains or embodies matter that meets the test of obscenity. 'Publish' has a wide meaning and is defined as including distributing, circulating, selling, giving, lending, and offering for sale or for lease. It seems clear that material posted to a newsgroup or published on a web page falls within the legal definition of publishing and is therefore covered by the Act. The publisher would appear to include the originator or poster of the item.

A.1.8 Telecommunications Act 1984

The transmission of an obscene or indecent image from one computer to another via a 'public telecommunications system' is an offence under s.43 of this Act. For traditional mail, the same sort of offence is created under the Post Office Act 1953.

A.1.9 Protection of Children Act 1978; Criminal Justice Act 1988

These Acts make it a criminal offence to distribute or possess scanned, digital or computer-generated facsimile photographs of a child under six years old that are indecent.

A.1.10 Copyright, Design and Patents Act 1998

Copyright law applies equally to the internet as it does to paper material. Many websites contain a copyright notice detailing how the material they contain may be used. Often, this is in the form of a hyperlink from a short copyright notice to a more detailed statement of what is permitted. If no copyright notice is provided, it is not safe to assume anything. If you want to print out a webpage or attachment, or copy and paste anything from a webpage or attachment into a document of your own, you should obtain the permission of the copyright owner. For any use beyond everyday web browsing, permission should be obtained. A good starting point is to send an email to the website operator. Where permission has not been granted, individuals and the Department could be liable to civil proceedings by the author.

A.1.11 Protection from Harassment Act 1997; Sex Discrimination Act 1975; Race Relations Act 1976

Harassment and discrimination are unlawful, whether or not the use of work-based communications facilities have played a role.

A.1.12 Computer Misuse Act 1990.

This Act makes it an offence for an unauthorised person to access knowingly a program or data or for such a person to modify knowingly the contents of a computer.

Annex 2 The Four Categories of Protective Marking: Definitions

A.2.1 Top Secret

The compromise of this information or material would be likely:

- to threaten directly the internal stability of the UK or friendly countries;
- to lead directly to widespread loss of life;
- to cause exceptionally grave damage to the effectiveness or security of UK or allied forces or to the continuing effectiveness of extremely valuable security or intelligence operations;
- to cause exceptionally grave damage to relations with friendly governments;
- to cause severe long-term damage to the UK economy.

A.2.2 Secret

The compromise of this information or material would be likely to:

- to raise international tension;
- to damage seriously relations with friendly governments;
- to threaten life directly, or seriously prejudice public order, or individual security or liberty;
- to cause serious damage to the operational effectiveness or security of UK or allied forces or the continuing effectiveness of highly valuable security or intelligence operations;
- to cause substantial material damage to national finances or economic and commercial interests.

A.2.3 Confidential

The compromise of this information or material would be likely to:

- materially damage diplomatic relations (cause formal protest or other sanction);
- to prejudice individual security or liberty;
- to cause damage to the operational effectiveness or security of UK or allied forces or the effectiveness of valuable security or intelligence operations;
- to work substantially against national finances or economic and commercial interests;
- substantially to undermine the financial viability of major organizations;
- to impede the investigation or facilitate the commission of serious crime;
- to seriously impede the development or operation of major government policies;
- to shut down or otherwise substantially disrupt significant national operations.

A.2.4 Restricted

The compromise of this information or material would be likely:

- to affect diplomatic relations adversely;
- to cause substantial distress to individuals;
- to make it more difficult to maintain the operational effectiveness or security of UK or allied forces;
- to cause financial loss or loss of earning potential to or facilitate improper gain or advantage for individuals or companies;
- to prejudice the investigation or facilitate the commission of crime;
- to breach proper undertakings to maintain the confidence of information provided by third parties;
- to impede the effective development or operation of government policies;
- to breach statutory restrictions on disclosure of information;
- to disadvantage government in commercial or policy negotiations with others;
- to undermine the proper management of the public sector and its operations.

Where it is necessary to indicate positively that an asset does not carry a protective marking, the term 'No Protective Marking' should be used.

Annex 3 Glossary

Abuse: *Inappropriate use of electronic facilities.*

Breach: *Contravention of Policy and Guidelines.*

Browser: *A software application used to locate and display Web pages.*

Chain Mail: *An electronic chain letter.*

Clear Desk Policy: *Departmental policy stating that all desks to be cleared of all documents to be stored securely each night.*

Content Monitoring: *The specific information about what was sent, received or processed through an electronic communication system.*

Devices: *Any electronic system used to send, receive or process information.*

Disciplinary Action: *Sanctions imposed by management, after investigation and due process, which could range from informal advice and warning, through suspension or demotion, to dismissal depending on the nature of the case.*

Download: *To copy to disk on a pc*

Electronic Communications: *Includes landlines and mobile telephones, fax machines, email, internet and PDAs.*

Email: *Electronic mail: that is, systems used to send or receive messages and attachments.*

Executable Programme: *Any file that can be run as a program. Usually ends in exe.*

GSI: *The external Government Secure Intranet – the UK Government network for information marked up to Restricted.*

Hardware: *PCs, telephones, fax machines and PDAs.*

Home Working: *Where an employee's home is their normal place of business.*

Inappropriate Material: *Any material of an offensive nature.*

Information Register: *A list of all protectively-marked documents taken offsite.*

Internet: *A network made up of worldwide networks with little control or management. Sometimes referred to as the World Wide Web.*

Intranet: *An internal network which is controlled and managed.*

ISO: *Information Security Officer.*

IT: *Information Technology.*

Malicious Software or executable programme: *Designed to deliver an undesirable effect , for example, viruses, worms, Trojan horse, and trapdoors.*

Manual of Protective Security Policy: *Guidelines and best practice issued to government departments by the Cabinet Office.*

Monitoring: *The process of analysing usage reports from electronic communication systems.*

Own Time: *Any time when the individual is not on duty.*

PCs: *Personal computers.*

PDAs Personal Digital Assistants: *Also known as palmtops or handheld pcs.*

Personal Use: *Usage of facilities that is not exclusively and necessarily in the performance of a user's official duties.*

Plug In: *An additional piece of hardware or software programme that adds a specific feature to a system.*

Protective Marking: *UK Government Standard for marking the value of all information , for example, Not Protectively Marked, Restricted, Confidential, Secret and Top Secret.*

Remote Working: *Away from your normal place of business , for example, at home, hotel or at a conference.*

Software: *Programmes and other operating information used by hardware.*

Traffic Monitoring: *The information processed through any electronic communication system , for example, who sent or received the information and when and where the information was sent or received.*

Upload: *To copy from disk to a network.*

Web Mail: *An email system provided by Internet Service Providers such as Hotmail.*

POLICY 2

LOG ON BANNER

REMEMBER !

The misuse of the email and internet across the Group is regarded as a serious breach of the Company's Data Protection Policy and Equal Opportunities Policy. The Group takes all misuse of its property and data protection and its equal opportunities policies very seriously and abuse of the system will result in serious disciplinary action including summary dismissal.

In particular, the accessing, downloading, distribution and viewing of illegal games, pornographic and/or other offensive material from the internet or the sending, viewing or distributing of offensive emails, whether in the form of pictures or words, is regarded as gross misconduct and could lead to summary dismissal.

Files including emails sent and received will be periodically reviewed by the Company, without warning, for non-business material and disciplinary action will be taken against anyone who breaches these Rules.

SO PLEASE DON'T DO IT !

REQUIRED READING – ON EMAIL AND INTRANET FIRST EDITION

19 March 2005

Internet Policy and Email Policy

1. Access to the internet and email system will be available to you for business use only. Use of these facilities will be monitored and disciplinary action may be taken if the facilities are abused or put to unsuitable use.

2. The prime use of this facility is for information and research. Access to certain sites may be withdrawn. User activity is monitored and logged. Copies of these logs are given to Compliance at regular intervals.

3. The downloading of any programme or wallpaper from the internet is strictly prohibited unless explicitly instructed to do so by the IT department. For example, this would include all shareware and freeware, particularly screen savers and desktop background patterns or wallpapers. Even if another user indicates he has IT approval, it is your personal responsibility to ensure you are complying with Company policy.

4. The deliberate downloading to or transmission from .... (or the deliberate use of .... property to download or transmit) pornographic, offensive, sexist, racist, defamatory or other material of a similar nature is a serious offence and will result in dismissal.

5. All downloaded attachments, for example, word documents that may contain word macros, must be virus scanned before opening.

6. If you are in any doubt regarding checking for viruses, contact the IT Helpdesk.

Email Policy

1. The guidelines and warnings listed below are of critical importance.
2. You are reminded that email is subject to the same Company policies as any other form of correspondence and should be used for business purposes only.
3. Beware what you say in email messages. Improper statements can give rise to personal or Company liability.
4. Assume that email messages may be read by others.
5. Messages that are abusive, sexist, racist or defamatory are never appropriate and must not be sent. It is a disciplinary offence to do so – regarded as gross misconduct for which summary dismissal is the normal penalty.
6. Always remember that email messages, however confidential or damaging, may have to be disclosed in court proceedings or in investigations by competition authorities/regulatory bodies if relevant to the issues. Remember that even if you have deleted an email message, a copy may still exist on back-up media or in other storage areas.
7. Never send strictly private and confidential messages by email unless prior consent has been obtained from the addressee. Confidential emails should be sent over the internet as encrypted files.
8. The content of all email messages is scanned automatically and logs are given to Compliance at regular intervals.
9. You are required to ensure that:
    - your email mailbox is checked at reasonable intervals for messages;
    - any messages found there are collected;
    - you must set appropriate access to your mailbox to cover both planned and unplanned absence.
10. Never import non-text files (for example, executable files, Word documents) or messages onto your system without having them scanned

for viruses or text bombs. If you have not been properly trained to scan for such viruses/bombs, the IT Helpdesk should be called to assist.

11. If you become aware of a virus warning, it should be referred to the IT Helpdesk only. Do not set about warning other internal and external bodies or individuals. If the virus warning is correct, then the IT Helpdesk will put out the usual warning email together with an entry in the Granite discussion group, with any specific instructions. If the warning is of the hoax type, you will be informed.
12. Make hard copies of emails, which you need to retain for record keeping purposes.
13. Always make hard copies of emails on client matters.
14. You must not enter into contractual commitments by email.
15. Do not create email congestion by sending trivial messages, unnecessarily copying/forwarding of emails , for example, chain mail letters, humorous stories or large attachments.
16. Do not advertise by email or send messages for missing items unless genuinely urgent for business reasons. Use the Newsgroups for the purpose.
17. Do not download, copy or transmit to third parties the works of others without their permission as this may infringe copyright.
18. Never send bank account or credit card information over the internet.
19. The following wording must precede the text when sending an external email:

The Company monitors and reads all emails as only business emails are permitted to be sent and received.

The Company also monitors emails for compliance reasons and to ensure that no unauthorized disclosure of confidential information is passed via the email system. This email and any attachments are confidential. It is intended for the recipient only. If you are not the intended recipient, any use, disclosure, distribution, printing or copying of this email is unauthorized. If you have received this email in error please immediately notify the sender by replying to this email and delete the email from your computer.

The contents of any attachment to this email may contain software viruses, which could damage your own computer system. While

.................plc has taken every reasonable precaution to minimise this risk, we cannot accept liability for any damage, which you sustain as a result of software viruses. You should carry out your own virus checks before opening the attachment.

Moves and Changes

1. All IT purchases by Division must be approved by the Group Head of IT (or in his absence by the Systems Manager) and must follow the Group policy on capital purchases.
2. A Change Control Form must be completed by a user or manager (and signed by their line manager) to request any move of part of the system or any change to the system (move of hardware, installation of software, change of login, removal of a user name, and so on), which could have an impact of another part of the system. Completed forms must be returned to the Helpdesk. Note that usernames will not be removed from the system until a Change Control form has been received requesting this to be done.
3. A New Starter form must be completed to request the creation of a user account for a new member of staff or a temporary member of staff. The form must be signed by a suitable manager and returned to the Helpdesk.

Logging Calls to the Helpdesk

1. All calls must be emailed to the Helpdesk using the email address helpdesk@.........com. If you are unable to email you can phone or fax the Helpdesk provided you email your query as soon as you are able to use email again. This is to ensure that a record is kept of all calls.
2. The request for support must contain:
    - the full details of the problem, for example, the applications running, the text of error messages, whether the problem is client/customer facing;
    - details of the urgency of the problem and a reasonable date and time when the problem should be fixed;
    - the text of the error messages and so on, whether the problem is client/customer facing.

POLICY 3

POLICY GOVERNING THE USE OF TELEPHONES, EMAIL AND THE INTERNET BY STAFF

Introduction

The provisions of this Policy apply to all members of staff, whether or not they have access to, or sole use of, a telephone or email/the internet on a personal computer.

These facilities are provided for Company business and it is recognized that the Company should provide guidance to employees about the appropriate use of telephones and email/internet access in order to safeguard the interests of both members of staff and the Company. Although access to such facilities does not form part of the benefits package of a member of staff, it is recognized that there are occasions when employees might legitimately make private use of their Company telephone to send or receive calls, use a computer to send and receive personal email and use their internet access for private use.

This Policy is intended to make clear what constitutes legitimate use in order that employees can use these facilities to their full potential on Company business and so that there is clarity about what does and does not constitute unacceptable use.

The Policy is not intended to place employees under unjustifiable scrutiny, but to give them a high measure of security and confidence about their use of email, telephones and the internet.

It should be noted that this Policy governs the use of telephones and email/internet access provided on personal computers or in computer clusters, to employees in order to allow them to undertake their employment. The fact that personal use of these facilities is in certain circumstances legitimate does not mean that such use is a formal benefit, nor does it give employees a right to such access. A number of jobs in the Company do not require access to these facilities and hence they are not provided.

The sections of the policy covered by misconduct and misuse should be read in conjunction with the appropriate staff disciplinary procedure as well as the IT Security Policy.

This Policy has been designed to safeguard the legal rights of members of staff under the terms of both the Data Protection Act and the Human Rights Act.

TELEPHONES

It is recognized that there will be occasions when employees need to make short, personal telephone calls on Company telephones, both fixed lines and mobiles, in order to deal with occasional and urgent domestic crises. (It should be emphasized that calls to mobile telephone numbers are particularly expensive and that these should be kept to an absolute minimum.)

Other personal calls should be made using public payphone facilities located on the campus in and outside of Company buildings or by use of personal mobile telephones. Alternatively, personal charge cards issued by the various telephone companies can be used on Company telephones to ensure that the cost of the call is charged to an individual's private account. Where possible, these non-urgent calls should be made during scheduled breaks or outside of the normal working day when they do not interfere with work requirements. Equally, it is legitimate to receive personal calls about domestic crises and arrangements, and occasional, short, non-urgent calls can be received providing they do not interfere adversely with work requirements.

For employees who do not have defined hours of work, such as senior members of staff, calls should not interfere, either by their timing or extent, with the performance of the employees' duties. The same rule applies to personal use of email and the internet, set out below, for this category of staff.

The use of Company telephones for either private or Company purposes, which are in any way excessive (that is, outside of the limits defined above), defamatory, obscene or otherwise inappropriate, will be treated as misconduct under the appropriate disciplinary procedure. In serious cases this could be regarded as gross misconduct and will lead to dismissal.

Where the Company has grounds to suspect possible misuse of its telephones, it reserves the right to monitor the destination and length of outgoing calls and the source and length of in-coming calls. This would not normally involve the surveillance of calls but in certain rare circumstances, where there are reasonable grounds to suspect serious misconduct, the Company reserves the right to record calls (see also recording of telephone calls and monitoring use of telephone, email and the internet below).

EMAIL

As with telephones it is recognized that employees can use email for personal means in certain circumstances. Email should be treated like any other form of written communication and, as such, what is normally regarded as unacceptable in a letter or memorandum is equally unacceptable in an email communication. It is legitimate for employees to make use of email outside of the normal working day for personal reasons to send messages that are in no sense obscene or defamatory or otherwise inappropriate.

For employees who do not have defined hours of work, such as senior members of staff, personal email use should not interfere, either by its timing or extent, with the performance of the employees' duties.

Employees should be careful that before they open any attachment to a personal email they receive, they are confident that the content is in no sense obscene or defamatory. Equally, if an employee receives an obscene or defamatory email, whether unwittingly or otherwise and from whatever source, they should not intentionally forward the email to any other address, except to an investigator in one of the computer support units. The matter should also be reported to the local users' support unit.

The use of email for either personal or Company purposes to send or forward messages or attachments which are in any way defamatory, obscene or otherwise inappropriate will be treated as misconduct under the appropriate disciplinary procedure. In serious cases this could be regarded as gross misconduct and will lead to dismissal.

Where the Company has reasonable grounds to suspect misuse of email in either scale of use, content or nature of messages, it reserves the right to monitor the destination, source and content of email to and from a particular address (see also recording of telephone calls and monitoring use of telephone, email and internet below).

The Company also reserves the right to access an employee's email account in their unexpected or prolonged absence (for example, due to sickness) in order to allow it to continue to undertake the employee's normal role. In normal circumstances the employee concerned will be contacted before this is done, in order to provide them with prior knowledge.

USE OF THE INTERNET

The primary reason for the provision of internet access is for the easy retrieval of information for research purposes in order to enhance the ability of its staff to undertake their role. However, as with email, it is legitimate for employees to make use of the internet in its various forms outside of normal working hours for personal purposes as long as it is not used to view or distribute improper material such as text, messages or images which are derogatory, defamatory or obscene.

It is recognized that there can be occasions where it is sensible for the employee to make occasional use of the internet for personal reasons such as a private transaction, rather than having to spend considerably more time out of the office. Examples of this might include a bank transaction or the booking of a holiday. As long as such personal use is confined to non-working hours, then it is permissible.

For employees who do not have defined hours of work, such as senior members of staff, personal internet use should not interfere, either by its timing or extent, with the performance of the employees' duties.

Unauthorised use of the internet will be treated as misconduct under the appropriate disciplinary procedure. In serious cases it could be treated as gross misconduct and could lead to dismissal.

The Company reserves the right to monitor the use of the internet from particular personal computers or accounts where it suspects misuse of the facility (see recording of telephone calls and monitoring use of telephone, email and internet below).

RECORDING OF TELEPHONE CALLS AND MONITORING OF USE OF TELEPHONE, EMAIL AND THE INTERNET

It is Company policy that no member of staff is permitted as a matter of routine to monitor a fellow employee's use of the Company's telephone or email service, or of the internet via the Company's networks. (The only exception is where designated Telephone Liaison Officers are authorised to receive print-outs of telephone call details from particular extensions for recharging purposes.)

However, as has been stated, where there are reasonable grounds to suspect an instance of misuse or abuse of any of these services, the Company

Secretary, the Director of Human Resources or in exceptional circumstances their duly authorised deputies, may grant permission for the recording of an employee's telephone calls and for the monitoring of use of telephones, email or the internet.

Once approved, the monitoring process will be undertaken by designated staff in Information Systems acting, for operational purposes, under the direction of the Director of Information Systems. These staff are required to observe the strictest confidentiality when undertaking these activities and they will record or monitor only to the extent necessary to establish the facts of the case. They will make their reports directly to the Director of Human Resources or his delegated representative, who, in consultation with the appropriate line manager, will determine the actions that may need to be taken in any particular case.

When monitoring is approved, the case for continued monitoring shall be reviewed on a regular basis with a view to terminating monitoring in as short a period of time as possible.

Staff who suspect misuse should in the first instance advise, in confidence, a member of the Human Resources team.

Index